T0116827

WHO MADE ENGLAND?

WHO MADE ENGLAND?

THE SAXON-VIKING RACE TO CREATE A COUNTRY

WRITTEN BY
CHIP COLQUHOUN

ILLUSTRATED BY
DAVE HINGLEY

The History Press

For Willow and Layla-Rose,
my beautiful nieces.

Chip

For my gorgeous wife, Vicki,
and our beautiful daughter Polly.

Dave

First published 2017
This edition published 2020

The History Press
97 St George's Place,
Cheltenham, Gloucestershire, GL50 3QB
www.thehistorypress.co.uk

British Library Cataloguing in Publication Data.
A catalogue record for this book is available from the British Library.

ISBN 978 0 7509 9374 6

Typesetting and origination by The History Press
Printed in Great Britain by TJ International, Ltd, Padstow, Cornwall

CONTENTS

ABOUT THE AUTHOR

CHIP COLQUHOUN began storytelling professionally in 2007, co-founding Epic Tales (formerly Snail Tales). He's since performed in eight countries, represented the Oxford Reading Tree online and written the EU's guide to storytelling for schools (available free from the Cambridgeshire Race Equality and Diversity Service). His first book for children was *Cambridgeshire Folk Tales for Children* (also published by The History Press), and his most recent was *The First King of England in a Dress* (published by Epic Tales). He lives in Cambridgeshire with Emma and Tito.

ABOUT THE ILLUSTRATOR

DAVE HINGLEY has always loved drawing and comic books. Since studying animation at the University of South Wales, Dave has worked in and around animation for the last eighteen years. He has recently produced illustrations for *Cambridgeshire Folk Tales for Children* and the stage show *The First King of England in a Dress*.

THANK YOUS FOR THE SECOND EDITION

Once again, I am deeply indebted to Nicola Guy, my commissioning editor at The History Press. Not only did she inspire the first edition of this book by inviting me to write *Cambridgeshire Folk Tales for Children*, but she lit the fire for this second edition to steam ahead. I couldn't have asked for a better editor to introduce me to the world of publishing!

The existence of this edition, though, also owes a lot to Dr Charles Insley, M.J. Trow and Carol. Over our long discussions prompted by the first edition, they helped me see where the book could be even more accurate. This may be written in a style that we hope all ages can access, but I never wanted that to be an excuse for it to be under researched! So big thanks to them all.

That same research was greatly helped along by Dr James Freeman, Dr Suzanne Paul and Prof Simon Keynes, each based at the University of

Cambridge. Great thanks to them all for their prompt assistance in my hours of need!

Thanks also to Berenice Mann, who helped me increase the accuracy of our reference to the Jewish nation.

Huge thanks again to Dave Hingley, for adding yet more illustrations to enliven the stories within these pages.

And finally, *mahoosive* thanks to my own Queen Emma, my kitten Tito and my father Paul – for their love, support and ice cream during my passions, projects and occasional panics.

FOREWORD FOR THE FIRST EDITION

How do you find out what's happening in the world?

You could ask your mum or dad. But how do *they* know what's happening? They may get the news from TV, websites or newspapers. And, of course, you can do the same.

Now imagine a world with no TVs, no computers, no newspapers. If you lived 1,000 years ago it would be *very* difficult to find out what was happening in the world. Your mum and dad wouldn't know any more than you, and chances are that none of you would be able to read or write.

That is the world that Chip writes about in this book. Studying history is like going on a journey with no satnav or map. All we have are a few clues to help us find our way. We have *facts*: information written long ago by the few people who could write. And we have *folklore*: stories told around the home fire as entertainment.

Chip has taken these two sources – fact and folklore – to tell us fascinating stories of the place we came to know as England. In this book you will meet people on your journey through time that you've never heard of before. They looked like us, although we don't know *exactly* what they looked like; they spoke a language we'd find hard to understand (although the word 'hard' is one we'd all recognise); and they had the same hopes and fears we still have today.

Because the most important people 1,000 years ago were the kings, Chip has written about them. What they did still matters, even after all this time, because they helped build the England we can see today.

M.J. Trow,
Historian and author

M.J. Trow wrote a biography of King Knut entitled Cnut: Emperor of the North. *You can watch M.J. and Chip looking at some of King Knut's letters in videos on* www.Kingdom1000.com

FOREWORD FOR THE SECOND EDITION

I wonder what it would be like to meet an English person from 1,000 years ago. We speak a language that was once like theirs, but I don't think we'd understand them today.

Some of the things they said, though, we might understand. They lived in a place that, by the year AD 1000, they called 'Engla Land' – not very far from our own 'England' – and some of the words and names around today are still very similar to what they would have been 1,000 years ago. If you're called 'Edward', that is a name that has not really changed in a millennium. Other Old English names, like 'Oswald' and 'Edmund', were common up until seventy years ago.

This was a world without radio, television or social media, where we have to piece together what happened from a few sources: documents written by the very small number of people who could write, and the things they left behind that archaeologists dig up for us. But we also have lots of stories that were told at the time, and which have come down to us as 'folklore'.

In this book, Chip has put together these sources to tell the exciting story of how England came to be one country, and the people – from England and from outside England – who made it.

Dr Charles Insley

Dr Insley is the Senior Lecturer in Medieval History at the University of Manchester. You can see him and Chip looking at some of the documentary evidence in videos on www.Kingdom1000.com

INTRODUCTION

Happy birthday!

Is it your birthday? If not, why not celebrate anyway? You were born on a day, right? So why not be as glad about it today as you would any other day?

A birthday means two things. First, it's a chance to celebrate! We hope to see our friends and family, get presents, and maybe even have a party.

But the second thing is something we can't escape (even though some people try): birthdays tell us our age.

Like birthdays, history has two meanings. The first is known as *folklore*. This has other names too – like legend, custom, or oral tradition – and it's partly why the subject is called hi*story*. It can be quite fun, like presents and parties.

We also have *historical facts*. These are things that can't change – like the date of your birthday.

Even so, facts can be hidden. Also, some things that *look* like facts can actually be lies – making it hard to find the truth.

Normally, history books look at only one type of history: fact *or* folklore. Most choose facts, perhaps because they think that's the best way to know the truth.

But is it really? Let's think about birthdays again. What's the best kind of present? Isn't it one where the person giving you the present has really thought about what you like?

In the same way, folklore can tell us about the characters in history, and what people thought of them. A story about someone may not be true. But if the story was told again and again by lots of different people, it shows us what they thought of that person. Someone popular would probably be a good character. Somebody no one likes, though, could become a bad guy.

For example, take King John. If you know any Robin Hood stories, you'll know that John is one of the bad guys. No one knows if Robin actually existed, but John certainly did. And the fact that John became a baddie for Robin shows that few people liked him.

Sometimes, facts and folklore say the same thing. For instance, facts say that John took English armies into battles they didn't win, and that English nobles forced John to make a *Magna Carta* (which simply means 'big agreement') saying that he wouldn't be such a bossy king. But the facts also tell us that John took armies to fight those nobles just a short while later – he didn't really care about that Magna Carta one bit.

But if we only had facts, how would we know what *ordinary* people thought about John? For many centuries, ordinary English people couldn't read or write, so they couldn't leave any facts for historians to know what *they* thought.

The only clues they could leave were the stories they told each other, again and again – until, many years later, someone *did* write them down.

So fact and folklore can *both* be useful for helping us make sense of history. That's why this book gives you both.

WHAT THIS BOOK'S ABOUT

This book is about England's 'birthday'. England has been an important country in history. Some of the world's most famous writers were born in England, such as Shakespeare and Jane Austen. England played a big part in stopping men who tried to take over the world, like Napoleon Bonaparte and Adolf Hitler. And people from England helped to build other countries like Australia and America.

But where did England come from? If we can find out, we could learn the secrets of its success – and avoid repeating some of its mistakes...

For a long time, though, England's birth was surrounded in mystery – partly because historians concentrated too much on *facts*. This meant that, instead of a proper history, we only had part of the picture.

Let's think about *your* birthday one more time. Imagine four friends come to your party, but only one of them gives you a present: a framed photo of you and them at a funfair.

Now imagine it's a few years later, and you haven't spoken to those friends in all that time. You've probably forgotten what they look like. But then you find that framed photo – so at least you can remember *that* friend. Wouldn't this make you think that they must have been your *best* friend, since they gave you something?

England's history was a bit like that. People knew there were many invasions – Romans, Saxons, Vikings, etc. But for a long time, one invasion was seen as the most important of all...

1066

In October 1066, a Norman duke called William invaded England. The English people had chosen someone called Harold to be their king, but William's army killed Harold at the Battle of Hastings.

William became King William I – though he's more often called 'William the Conqueror'. Maybe that name suits him better, because he didn't stop attacking the English even after beating Harold. He took his army east to attack ordinary English people there, and also marched north – setting fire to the farms and homes of ordinary people as he went.

But William and his Normans weren't just good at attacking. They were also good at writing things down. William's most famous book (though he didn't write it himself) is known as the *Domesday Book*, and it's the first book to record facts about what was going on in England at the time it was being written.

Maybe that's why the Norman invasion was, for a long time, considered the most important invasion of all: this was when facts from English history began to get written down *properly*.

However, as we said a few pages ago, there is a problem with concentrating too much on facts:

things can get hidden. And a good example is the *Domesday Book*.

You see, this was written to let William know exactly where to find all the money in England. That way, he could prove just how rich and powerful he was.

We don't have that proof for the kings before William. Perhaps some of those kings were richer and more powerful than William. But we can't know for sure, because the only king with a detailed book about his power is William.

So, for a long time, people who thought history was all about *facts* believed that the history of England only really began from 1066.

This also meant that, for just as long a time, a lot of people (including history teachers in schools) believed that William was the first *important* king of England. And in some ways he was – he's the ancestor of nearly every king and queen of England since then. Even Queen Elizabeth II is William's great-granddaughter!

That's why schools used to teach the kings and queens of England in a poem that began with William:

Willie Willie Harry Stee,
Harry Dick John Harry three;
One two three Neds, Richard two
Harrys four five six... then who?
Edwards four, five, Dick the bad,
Harrys twain and Ned the lad;
Mary, Bessie, James the Vain,
Charlie, Charlie, James again...
Will and Mary, Anna Gloria,
Georges four, Will four, Victoria;
Edward seven next, and then
George the fifth in nineteen ten;
Ned the eighth soon abdicated
Then George the six was coronated;
And if you've not yet lost your breath,
Give a cheer for the second Elizabeth!

But hold on. Do we really want William the Conqueror to be the first king we remember? True, he was a successful invader. But isn't it dangerous to call him the first important king, when he also killed a lot of ordinary people in the years *after* his invasion?

You see, other men tried to copy what William did. We've mentioned a couple of them already: Napoleon and Hitler. I'm sure you know what happened to at least one of them...

William may have actually been a bit of a bully. He attacked England when it was weak, then tried to make it turn completely Norman – getting rid of anything that was 'different'.

But England only became strong enough to beat Napoleon and Hitler when its rulers tried bringing people together instead. For example, Queen Elizabeth I brought Catholics and Protestants together, and her England beat the Spanish Armada. King Charles II brought the Royalists and Parliamentarians together, and his England produced some of the world's most important scientists, like Sir Isaac Newton. Queen Anne brought England and Scotland together to make Great Britain, and that soon became one of the world's richest countries.

Elizabeth, Charles and Anne were following an example set by some of the kings and queens from *before* William – the ones you'll meet in this book.

By the way, in case you're now worrying that Queen Elizabeth II is the great-great-(etc.)-granddaughter of a bully, there is some good news: she has another great-great-(etc.)-grandfather who you'll meet in this book, and *he* was much more interested in bringing people together...

But more on that later.

WHEN WAS ENGLAND BORN?

It may sound obvious to say that England had a 'birthday'. After all, everything starts somewhere, right?

Actually, though, it's not that easy. The first problem is that there's no *fact* to tell us the date of England's 'birthday'. The second problem is more complicated: *people understand history differently*.

If this book was about the history of America, we wouldn't have the first problem. There are papers saying America was born on the 4th of July 1776, when the people living there made a 'Declaration of Independence'. Nowadays, every 4th of July, America remembers its birthday with a celebration called Independence Day.

But we might still have the second problem, even though the Declaration of Independence is a fact. That's because some people say America really started when Christopher Columbus discovered the land on the 12th of October 1492. Others say it began when English, French and Spanish families started arriving from 1600. Yet others say America first got its name from a German map in 1507!

You see, there are lots of ways to understand history. And English history is even harder than

American history, because no one has ever found a Declaration of Independence for England.

Plus, facts tell us that English people were around before England had been invented.

'WAIT... WHAT?!'

That's right: English people didn't come from England.

Around 1,500 years ago, the first people to be called English were the *Angles* – invaders from part of the world we now call Germany.

Do you see? The proper way to say Angles is *Ang-les*, which sounds a bit like saying *Anglish* – and that would eventually become *English*.

This may surprise you, but it's actually not unusual – even today. People living in the European Union may call themselves European, even though Europe isn't a country. The United Kingdom *is* a country, and people who live there are called British, but there are still people who call themselves English, Scottish, Welsh, or Irish.

Then there's the Jewish nation. Today, there is a Jewish country called Israel; once, there was a Jewish country called Judah. Both these countries took their names from Jewish men who travelled the ancient world. Wherever you live today, you can make friends with Jewish people. They aren't from just one country – they are a group of people sharing the same religion.

So your nationality can depend on the land you come from, but it can depend on other things too – like religion, history, or even just how you feel.

It helps to remember the difference between a country and a nation. A *country* is an area of land, but a *nation* is a group of people. That's how the English *nation* could be around before there was a *country* called England.

As you'll discover in this book, England was made with the help of quite a few different men and women. Many of them were English, but just as many were Saxons – and a few came from other places.

So who finished the job?

HOW TO USE THIS BOOK

This book will help you make up *your* mind about the big questions we've looked at so far: 'Who made England?' and 'What can we learn from the creation of England?'

We'll look at several characters who shaped the country that would eventually be called England. For each one, we'll discover some *facts* about them. But we'll also have some *folklore*. This will help us know what people at the time thought about the people in charge – and that might help us understand *why* things happened the way they did.

Then, after we've looked at a character, you'll find a summary of what they did, followed by two scoresheets like this:

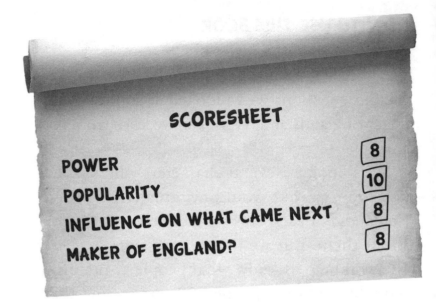

SCORESHEET

POWER   8

POPULARITY   10

INFLUENCE ON WHAT CAME NEXT   8

MAKER OF ENGLAND?   8

Each category is scored out of ten. One scoresheet will be completed by me, but the other is for *you* to fill. As we saw, how we understand history can differ from person to person – and you are very much allowed to have your own opinion. So write in what *you* think!

Chip Colquhoun,
May 2017

WHERE DID THE ENGLISH COME FROM?

We've already looked at how the word *English* came from the Angles, one of the groups of people (or *tribes*) who invaded Britain after the Romans.

This tribe came from a small country somewhere in the middle of Europe, which was called *Angel* (not a shiny man with wings – it's pronounced *Ang-gel*). Since this country was part of the land we now call Germany, historians call them a *Germanic tribe*.

The Angles arrived in Britain around the same time as another Germanic tribe: the Saxons, who came from *Saxony*.

Other Germanic tribes came to Britain too, such as the Jutes – but the Angles and Saxons are the most famous. Because they all came from the same area of Europe, they all spoke a very similar language to each other (if you speak German, you'd have a good chance of understanding them!).

But why did these tribes come here in the first place? And where exactly is 'here'? After all, we can't exactly call it England yet...

THE LAND OF WHATCHAMA-CALL-IT

When people first came to the land of England, long before the Angles and Saxons, the word *England* didn't exist. Some historians still call it England anyway, because that's what it would become. But for our quest that would be confusing – it would be like naming a baby before its grandmother has been born!

Instead, let's use the name the Romans gave this land: *Britain*.

People once thought Britain was named after a famous Roman soldier called Brutus, but most historians today don't believe Brutus was a real person. It could be that Britain sounded closer to the name that the *Celts* had for the land. The Celts lived in Britain before the Romans, and there are still some Celtic languages around today: like *Welsh*. In Wales, the land is called *Prydain* – which sounds a bit like Britain beginning with a P.

Wherever it came from, that name stuck. In fact, we're still using it today, over 2,000 years later. The Romans called the Celts who lived there *Britons* – and we still use that word today too, for *anyone* who is now born in Britain.

WHY DID THE ANGLES AND THE SAXONS ARRIVE?

Around AD 410, the Roman leaders left Britain. Their Empire was collapsing, and they probably wanted to go back to their own lands around Italy. Those left behind were a mixture of ordinary Roman Britons and Celtic Britons – including a Celtic tribe in the north known as the Scots.

The Romans were scared of the Scots. The Roman Emperor Hadrian had built a huge wall at the bottom of Scotland to try and keep them out. But when the Roman leaders left, they took their best soldiers with them – so now the Scots kept coming through Hadrian's Wall to attack the Roman Britons who were left behind.

A book from near this time says this is why the Saxons came over: the Roman Britons asked them for help fighting the Scots.

But we will never know for sure if this is fact or folklore. Although it was written down, it was written by a monk called Gildas as part of a sermon, and he may have made it up. One of the clues is his 'happy ending': Gildas says the Romans will return to get rid of the Saxons. We now know this didn't happen – the Saxons stayed in Britain, and are still there today!

Why would Gildas make up this story? Well, if you go to church, you may hear the vicar telling a story to help make a point. So it's possible Gildas made up this story to teach the moral, 'Don't ask devils to help you fix a problem.'

The Roman Britons probably thought the Angles and Saxons were devils because they quickly beat the Roman British soldiers and took over the land. Since these Germanic tribes were so keen to build homes in Britain, some historians think they invaded because lands like Angel and Saxony were too small.

The other Celtic Britons didn't all go away. Many ended up in the land we now call *Wales*. These Celts must have been quite fierce too, because one of the first Saxon kings – King Offa – dug a long, wide ditch between Wales and his kingdom, Mercia. Known as *Offa's Dyke*, this ditch was made for almost the same reason as Hadrian's Wall.

THE SEVEN GERMANIC KINGDOMS OF BRITAIN

After arriving in Britain, the Germanic tribes soon carved up the land into seven different countries (see the map in the picture). Because each country was ruled by its own king, we call them *kingdoms*. Some were home to Saxons, some to Angles, and still others to Jutes.

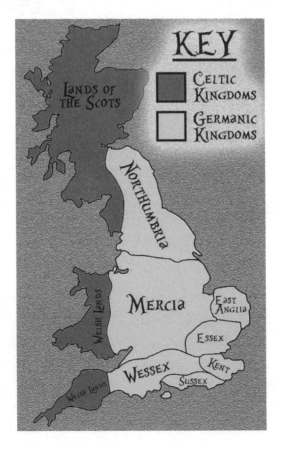

Since these tribes all spoke a similar language, they *could* be friendly with each other. For example, a Saxon princess might get married to an Angle prince.

But some of the kings wanted to be the best king in Britain, so they often started wars with each other. After a war, the winning king wouldn't always kill the loser. Instead, he might force the loser to call him *overlord*.

Some got so good at winning wars that they became the overlord for *all* seven kingdoms – such as King Egbert of Wessex around AD 830.

But Egbert didn't think to stick all the kingdoms together to make just one. Instead, he preferred to have everyone calling him overlord. He was basically the king of all kings!

Doesn't 'king of all kings' sound more powerful than just 'king'? Perhaps that's why Egbert didn't bother sticking all his kingdoms together.

But, because he didn't, the kingdoms soon split up again after he died, each again ruled by its own king.

THE VIKINGS

By the end of the ninth century, the Angles and the Saxons probably felt pretty good about themselves. They ruled seven kingdoms spread all over Britain, and sometimes ruled the Scots and Welsh too.

Then the Vikings arrived.

Vikings came from the northern part of Europe often called Scandinavia. They were actually made up of several Germanic nations: Danes, Norse, and more. But they all had one thing in common: they *hated* the Saxons. You might wonder why – after all, they had all once been Germanic tribes, so they all spoke a similar language. They even had some of the same gods, though with slightly different names (for example, Saxons told stories about *Woden*, and Vikings told the same stories about *Odin*).

But there was a time, long before Vikings came to Britain, when the Saxons were the fiercest warriors in Europe – and Vikings were scared of them. So scared, in fact, that Vikings built something like Hadrian's Wall to keep them out! Known as the *Danevirke*, it can still be seen in north Germany today.

So when the Angles and Saxons in Britain began fighting each other to prove who had the most powerful king, perhaps the Vikings attacked because their enemy was now split up, and they saw a chance to get revenge?

At first, all the Vikings did was sail over in huge boats, plunder the Angles and Saxon towns to steal treasure, then sail away again. But Britain clearly had a lot of treasure, because there was always more to find – and this gave some Vikings the idea to stay in Britain. They could get even richer that way.

But this meant the Vikings began fighting the Angles and Saxons not just for money, but to rule the kingdoms. One of the first kingdoms to become a Viking country was Northumbria, but many others quickly succumbed to the Vikings too. Eventually, there was only one Saxon kingdom left: Wessex.

However, just like the Angles and Saxons, winning Vikings didn't *always* kill the English losers. Sometimes they just forced those kings to accept a Viking overlord. So the seven kingdoms were still there, dividing the land of Britain between several rulers.

LIFE IN A SAXON/VIKING KINGDOM

Between battles, life for ordinary people could continue as normal.

In those days, most ordinary people in Britain worked on farms. Sheep were popular animals, since they gave food, milk, and wool (warm clothes were important – Britain was even colder then than it is now!).

The next biggest job was blacksmithery: making things out of metal. Blacksmiths made everything from weapons, like swords, to household objects, like chamber pots – these were small pots to use as a toilet!

Most ordinary people lived in huts with only one room, where they slept on rugs, cooked on open fires, ate at tables... and used their chamber pots.

Children in those times helped their parents with their jobs. They still had toys, like dolls, spinning tops and even board games like *taefl* (a bit like chess) – but they had to make them first, usually out of wood.

Adults had fun too – like horse racing or dancing. Women danced to celebrate events like birthdays, while men danced to keep fit – in case they got called to become soldiers.

All men were soldiers. If their king decided to fight another king, or if their country came under attack, every man had to pick up a sword.

It was more or less the same whether you were Angles, Saxon, or Viking. The main difference was the law. In Angles and Saxon kingdoms, if you had a problem with someone, you went to the most powerful man in your town (sometimes the king, but sometimes a noble) and asked him to sort it out. If you had lots of friends who agreed with you, then you were more likely to win.

You may think this wasn't fair, since whoever had the most friends would *always* win – and perhaps a rich man could bribe people to be his friends. But Viking rules weren't very fair either: if you had a problem with someone, you'd fight them! So the *strongest* Viking always won.

For the most part, though, people tried to live together peacefully. They did this because it was safer, of course, but also because many were becoming Christians.

THE IMPORTANCE OF CHRISTIANITY

Christianity became popular thanks to the same thing that helped William the Conqueror convince many historians that he was the first important king in England: *writing*.

You see, Christianity really took off when Romans became Christians. Romans loved to write, and kept very good records of things that happened in their Empire. Even when the Roman Empire collapsed, many Christians kept writing. This helped them become some of the cleverest people in the world – it's easier to remember things if you write them down. That's why many people think reading and writing are two of the most important skills you can learn, even today.

So back in the ninth century, people looked up to the monks: Christian men who lived in churches called monasteries, and learned to read and write. In fact, the first England-maker we'll meet was a monk...

BEDE

Around AD 680, a boy arrived at a monastery in Northumbria, ready to live with the monks for a few months. Maybe he didn't think he would become a monk himself – at first, his reason for being there was just to learn. In those days, monks were schoolteachers too.

This boy was Bede. He was an Angle, but Bede is partly responsible for people thinking of Angles and Saxons as the *Anglo-Saxons* today – all

because he wrote one of the first books to come out of Britain: *The Ecclesiastical History of the English People.*

WHO WAS BEDE?

Most of what we know about Bede actually comes from that book. He says one of his teachers was a monk called Ceolfrith, and we know from another old book that Ceolfrith was one of only two monks who survived the plague in his monastery. The other monk was apparently a boy – so perhaps that boy was Bede? If so, this is a clue that Bede became a monk very early in his life.

Bede helped with jobs around the monastery like cooking and cleaning, but he also really enjoyed singing. According to a letter by one of his friends, Bede died singing!

Like the monks who taught him, Bede became a teacher. He wrote some of his teachings down, and wrote songs too. Most of these have sadly been lost, but one book survived to become very famous...

THE ECCLESIASTICAL HISTORY OF THE ENGLISH PEOPLE

Ecclesiastical means 'to do with Christians'. Bede's book was mainly about how Christianity came to Britain.

Being a monk, Bede tried to explain why things happened by thinking of what God must have wanted. For instance, he began his book with the story of the Romans bringing Christianity to Britain for the first time. After the Roman leaders left and the Saxons arrived, Bede was angry that the Roman Britons didn't share their Christianity with the Saxons. That's why Bede thought the Saxons were able to take over most of Britain: God was punishing the Roman Britons for keeping Christianity to themselves.

Bede then described how monks brought Christianity back to Britain, starting with the Jutes in Kent, then the Angles in Northumbria, and eventually the Saxons in Sussex.

What's this got to do with making England? Well, have a look at the title again: *The Ecclesiastical History of the ENGLISH People*. Now look at the last paragraph. Bede writes about Christianity spreading to the Jutes, Angles, and Saxons.

So Bede was the first person to write as if everyone living in Britain was part of the same nation: the Angles! As we saw in the introduction, *Angles* would become the word *English*. Bede thought this even though Britain was still split into different kingdoms, full of people from different parts of Europe.

Bede thought everyone in Britain was part of one nation because they all shared one *religion* – a bit like the Jewish nation, who didn't start with a country of their own but *did* all pray to the same God.

Perhaps it's no surprise that Bede decided the name of the united nation should be Angles – after all, he was an Angle himself!

THE INVENTION OF 'ENGLAND'?

Bede didn't believe all Angles and Saxons lived in the same country – far from it. He knew there were different kingdoms all over Britain, from Kent in the south up to Northumbria in the north.

However, in the year AD 897 (about 150 years after Bede died) a Saxon in Wessex was translating Bede's *Ecclesiastical History* from Latin into the language of the Saxons. Translated into *modern* English, Bede had written something like this:

'The church of Abercorn is in the land of the English, but near the sea...'

But when the Saxon translated this into the Saxon language, he made a mistake. If we translate his mistake into modern English, we get something like this:

'The church of Abercorn is in England, but near the sea...'

So the first time the word *England* was ever used, it was a spelling mistake! Perhaps that Saxon was rushing to finish his translation too fast...

This Saxon was copying Bede's book for Alfred the Great. Even so, the word 'England' didn't catch on yet – because there wasn't one country called England in 897, and there wouldn't be one for over another 100 years.

Was it an easy mistake to make? When Bede wrote 'the land of the English', didn't he mean all seven of the Anglo-Saxon kingdoms that would eventually stick together to make England?

Maybe that's why some historians think Bede helped make the country of England. How big a 'Maker of England' score would *you* give him?

SUMMARY

Bede made it look as if everyone in the seven Anglo-Saxon kingdoms was part of the same family, even though they came from different parts of Europe. He did this because he wanted them all to pray to the Christian God. But he called them *English* (or *Ang-les*) because that was *his* tribe. If Bede had been a Saxon, perhaps England would today be called Saxonland?

We don't have any folklore about Bede, but we can tell from his writing that he wanted everyone to feel they were on the same side. That wasn't just a nice thing about his personality – it would also influence a certain king called Alfred...

AUTHOR'S SCORESHEET

POWER   6

POPULARITY   7

INFLUENCE ON WHAT CAME NEXT   7

MAKER OF ENGLAND?   6

YOUR SCORESHEET

POWER

POPULARITY

INFLUENCE ON WHAT CAME NEXT

MAKER OF ENGLAND?

ALFRED THE GREAT

In AD 849, a prince was born in the Saxon kingdom of Wessex. Although his father was a Christian, the boy was named after a creature of legend: 'Alfred' means 'wise elf'.

Elves may not really exist, but Prince *Alfred* was destined to become a legend...

FOLKLORE: THE BOY WHO WOULD BE KING

Alfred was the son of King Ethelwulf. Soon after Alfred was born, Ethelwulf travelled to Rome to meet the Pope. A lot of kings did this, from all over the world, because the Pope represented the Christian God. If the Pope liked you, it meant God must like you – and *everybody* had to like you if God was on your side!

The Pope at the time was Leo IV. He probably met Ethelwulf in the middle of one of Rome's great halls, surrounded by guards in armour, nobles in fine dresses, and servants holding trays of sweet foods and wine.

During the meeting, Ethelwulf picked up his young son and showed him to Leo. 'Your Holiness, may I introduce you to the new prince of Wessex: Alfred.'

Leo smiled gently at first. But suddenly his eyes widened and he felt a tingle down his back – something that often happened when God wanted to speak through him. Almost by itself, Leo's hand rose up and lightly touched Alfred's forehead.

With a voice that everyone in that huge hall could hear, Leo announced: 'Alfred. By the grace of God – you *will* be king.'

IS IT TRUE?

This story is found in an ancient book called the *Anglo-Saxon Chronicle*, which was written while Alfred was king. The *Chronicle* isn't as detailed as the *Domesday Book*, and it's certainly not as detailed as most history books written today.

But, like the *Domesday Book*, it was written by friends of the king – so it was probably going to say nice things about him. We've already seen how the *Domesday Book* made William the Conqueror look like the most powerful king anyone had ever seen. Alfred may have been pleased with the *Chronicle* telling this story – surely Alfred was powerful if God said he would be king!

There is another piece of evidence for this story: a letter from Pope Leo himself. But he doesn't say Alfred will be king: instead, he calls him a *consul*. This was an important job too, a bit like being a judge, so Alfred could still tell people what to do.

Perhaps the writer of the *Chronicle* just misunderstood what Leo meant. That may have been an easy mistake to make. After all, Leo probably spoke Latin – the writer of the *Chronicle* spoke Saxon.

FOLKLORE: THE MIND OF A KING

Alfred's mother, Queen Osburh, loved reading to her children – and they loved listening to her. Her sing-song voice made Saxon poems sound like delightful music.

But Osburh knew she couldn't read to her children forever. Eventually they would have to learn to read themselves. So one day, Osburh held her children's favourite book – one with beautiful illustrations at the start of each poem – and said, 'Now children, you know that books aren't just about pretty pictures, don't you? It's important to know what the words mean.'

One prince sat up straighter. 'But I really like the pictures in that book!'

'Really?' replied Osburh. 'Would you like to look at it whenever you want?'

All her children called out, 'Yeah!'

Osburh smiled. 'Well then, we'll have a competition. The first one of you who learns to read this book to me can keep it!'

For a moment the children looked excited, but then their smiles disappeared. None of them could read yet – the competition would be hard.

But then Osburh's youngest son put his hand up. 'Mummy... will you *really* give that book to the first one who understands and repeats it to you?'

Osburh nodded. 'Yes, Alfred.'

Before Osburh or the others could do anything, Alfred stood up and took the book from her hands, then ran out of the room.

Alfred's sister stared after him. 'Do you really think he can learn all those words?'

One of Alfred's brothers shook his head. 'No chance. He's too little.'

*

Alfred plonked the book on the desk of his schoolteacher, a monk. 'Please sir, can you read this to me?'

The monk looked confused. 'Isn't that the book your mother reads to you?'

Alfred nodded. 'Yes. I want to learn it. Please read it over and over – but slowly, so I can repeat it after you.'

The monk frowned. 'That's not what learning means, Alfred. You'll remember it, yes. But learning is not the same as remembering. If you learn to read, you'll be able to read other books too.'

Alfred thought for a moment, then said, 'That's true. But if I hear the words first, I'll understand them more, and that will make my mind bigger. And if my mind gets bigger, I'll be better at learning things. So if you start by teaching me with your voice, eventually I'll be even better at learning to read.'

Now the monk smiled. 'Alfred, you're already thinking like a reader. Alright – I'll read it for you.'

*

When Alfred finished reciting the last poem from the book, everyone in the room was silent for a moment. His brothers and sister all had their jaws hanging down as far as they could go.

Then Osburh clapped. One at a time, his sister and brothers joined in.

Chuffed, Alfred held the book out for his mother.

But Osburh just shook her head. 'No, Alfred. You won: the book is yours.'

IS IT TRUE?

This story comes from a book by one of Alfred's friends – a monk called Asser. That doesn't mean the story is true. Asser wasn't in Wessex when Alfred was a boy, so he must have heard the story from someone else. Even if he heard it from Alfred, it might not be completely true. After all, Alfred may have wanted people to hear this story because it makes him look like he was always really clever.

ALFRED THE LEAST

Whether or not the folklore so far has been true, it was probably still a surprise that Alfred became king. All Alfred's brothers were older than him – and all four were kings before him.

When Alfred was born, his family were already powerful Saxons. His grandfather was King Egbert – remember him from two chapters ago? He had been overlord of all the Anglo-Saxon kingdoms. Although Alfred's father Ethelwulf didn't control as many kingdoms, he still ruled Kent as well as Wessex.

About this time, though, Vikings began attacking. Ethelwulf lost a couple of battles to them – but, for the first twenty-one years of Alfred's life, Wessex was one of the safest places to be. That is until Alfred's third brother became king. Then the Vikings came with a huge army. They had already taken over Northumbria, East Anglia, Essex and Mercia – Wessex was next.

The Wessex Saxons won *some* battles against the Vikings. One of Alfred's friends even wrote that Alfred's leadership was the reason the Saxons won the Battle of Ashdown.

However, the Vikings won *most* of the battles. After Alfred became king, Viking attacks continued for seven years until, eventually, they managed to defeat Alfred's army. To survive, Alfred had one choice: run away.

So, at about twenty-nine years old, Alfred was king of the last Saxon kingdom in the whole of Britain – and he had to hide. He probably didn't feel very 'Great' at that point...

FOLKLORE: ALFRED AND THE CAKES

This tale begins just a short while after a Viking called Guthrum destroyed Alfred's last army in AD 878.

The people of Wessex were sad. They had lost their king. Without Alfred, there was no point fighting the Vikings. They tried to get on with their lives, but a lot of their food and money was taken by the Vikings – so nearly every Saxon family was left poor and starving.

Alfred saw all of this. He wandered the villages of Wessex disguised as a beggar, hiding his face. It would be dangerous to show himself to anyone – if the Vikings found out where he was, they might set the whole village on fire.

But Alfred became desperately hungry. Eventually he *had* to go to someone's hut and ask for food.

The first door he knocked on opened very slightly, and a peasant woman peered through the gap. 'Who are you?'

Alfred wanted to say, 'I am your king!' But the fear in her eyes stopped him. He didn't want her to carry his big secret – that would only add to her worries.

So instead Alfred just said he was a Saxon soldier, who had only just escaped the Vikings.

Now the woman smiled at him. 'If you fought the Vikings, you've already suffered enough. Come inside. You're lucky, actually – I'm baking some cakes.'

Knowing that his people were kind-hearted instantly made Alfred feel better – though probably not as much as the cakes were going to! They were baking on a grill over the fire in the middle of her hut, smelling delicious. Alfred went over and sat by the fire, enjoying its heat.

The woman turned the cakes over with some tongs. Then she suddenly looked at Alfred with excited eyes. 'Oh! My husband asked me to fetch some mead for him before he got back from the fields – but I haven't been able to leave yet, in case the cakes burnt. Could you watch them for me?'

Alfred took the tongs from her. 'Kind lady, I would do anything for you.'

The woman left, and Alfred held the tongs ready to turn the cakes if they began to get too brown. As he watched, the flames flickered – just like the flames that had surrounded his last fortress...

Alfred stared at those flames. As they danced around each other, he remembered his soldiers fighting the Vikings. The attack had been a surprise: the Viking leader Guthrum had shaken Alfred's hand, pretending to leave in peace, but then ordered his army to attack again before the Saxons could prepare. If only Alfred had seen it coming...

The flames rose higher. As they did, they created a new picture in Alfred's mind. Many armies of Saxons, rising up from all over Wessex. Alfred's eyes widened. Of course! His main army had been defeated, but there were soldiers guarding nobles all over Wessex. If he could find a way to bring them together without the Vikings finding out, then *he* could surprise *them*!

A plan was forming in his mind. The woman had shown him how Saxons trusted each other – so he would trust them too. He would find ordinary Saxons to be his spies, sneaking around Wessex with secret messages. No Viking would suspect an ordinary peasant travelling to buy wool for their clothes. But those peasants could let Alfred's nobles know he was alive, and tell them all to gather at exactly the same place and time.

But where? The smell of hot metal reminded Alfred of stone... Egbert's Stone! Where better to bring the Saxons together than the marker of the last king who ruled all the Saxon kingdoms?

But when? The flames brightened, their forked tongues whipping from cake to cake, reminding Alfred of the moment in the Bible when fire from Heaven touched each disciple of Jesus to give them gifts of the Holy Spirit: the festival of

Whitsunday. Yes! Alfred's forces would gather on Whitsunday!

Alfred leaned back, satisfied. This time it would be the *Viking* fortresses burning. He could smell it now – their burning armour, their panicked wails, their shouts of 'What have you done to my cakes?'

No, wait. That wasn't right...

Alfred snapped out of his daydream. The smell wasn't of burning armour – it was of burning cakes! And the panicked wail was from the peasant woman, who threw a bucket of water over the flames. Now just a few black lumps lay hissing on the grill. They looked more like coal than cakes.

The woman glared at Alfred. 'I trusted you! I asked you to do *one* simple thing – and you sat there like a walnut! What were you *thinking*?'

For a moment, Alfred wanted to shout back, 'I was thinking about saving Wessex, woman! You will *not* talk to your king like that!'

But Alfred knew the woman had a right to be angry. By burning those cakes, Alfred had ruined her whole day's work. So instead, Alfred looked down at his feet. 'I'm sorry, dear lady. You're right – I should have paid attention, especially when you trusted me. I am a terrible king.'

'Too right!' spat the woman. But suddenly her mouth dropped open wide enough to bounce an apple inside. 'You said "king"?'

Alfred gave her a shy smile, and nodded slowly.

The woman dropped to her knees and bowed deeply. 'Your Majesty! I am so sorry!'

But Alfred helped her to her feet. 'Good lady, please don't apologise. You did nothing wrong. I *did* get distracted. And I am deeply grateful to you. You helped me work out how we can make the Saxons great again.'

The woman looked puzzled. 'I did?'

Alfred nodded. 'You showed me just how much we can trust each other, and how good Saxons can be if they work together.'

The woman's face lightened with hope. 'We can get Wessex back?'

'Not just Wessex,' replied Alfred. 'Think how powerful we'll be if *all* the Vikings' enemies unite! Saxons, Angles, and Jutes... We'll be unstoppable! The Vikings won't stand a chance!'

IS IT TRUE?

Most historians think this story is just a story. It's been told in so many different ways that no one really knows where it came from. The only truths we know for sure are that Alfred hid from the Vikings for a while, then chose Whitsunday for a surprise attack on the Vikings.

One clue that it *isn't* true is that Alfred's friend Asser didn't put it in his book about Alfred's life. But then, maybe Alfred didn't want him to – perhaps he thought it made him look a bit silly.

Still, this story suggests that Alfred really cared about saving his people – so much so that he couldn't concentrate on anything else.

It also makes Alfred look like a *humble* king. The woman got angry with him, but he just bowed his head and apologised.

Perhaps that's the main reason why this story lasted so long: people liked the idea of a king who knew how to say sorry. He wasn't a bully – he could be a friend as well as a king.

FOLKLORE: ALFRED THE MINSTREL

As Alfred gathered the remaining Saxon soldiers in Wessex, he knew he needed more than just surprise on his side. He needed to know how Vikings *thought*.

So Alfred disguised himself as a minstrel – a travelling musician – with an instrument called

a lyre (kind of like a harp, but the same size as a guitar). Then he walked right into the camp where Guthrum, the Viking leader, was celebrating with his men – and offered to sing for them.

Alfred was such a good singer that the Vikings loved his music. Guthrum had met Alfred a few times, but still didn't recognise him. He just sat and enjoyed the music alongside the rest of his men.

Lyres only had six strings, one for each note – so Alfred had to retune the strings before each new song. While he did this, he also listened to everything Guthrum and the Vikings said to each other. He heard them discuss their favourite battle formations, problems with their weapons, how Alfred was probably dead...

After Alfred's final song, the Vikings gave him a huge round of applause. He bowed silently, then walked straight back to the Saxon camp.

Throwing off his disguise, Alfred smiled at his men.

'Beating the Vikings will be easy. Here's what we have to do...'

IS IT TRUE?

This story was first written down in AD 1125 – about 250 years after it would have happened.

It was written by William of Malmesbury – and many historians trust William to tell the truth. His books include details about the Saxons that we can't find anywhere else, but also a lot of details we *can* find elsewhere. If we know a large part of what he writes is true, surely some of the rest is true too? So even though we can't find the story of 'Alfred the Minstrel' in a book before William, that doesn't mean William made it up.

Either way, this story gives us even more information about what people thought Alfred was like: a talented singer, and very brave – think what the Vikings would have done if they'd seen through his disguise!

It's also true that Alfred won his next battle against Guthrum's Vikings, the Battle of Ethandun. Was this because Alfred surprised the Vikings? Was it because Alfred had listened to their plans while tuning his lyre? Was it a mixture of both these reasons?

WHAT MADE ALFRED GREAT?

When Alfred finally beat Guthrum's Vikings, he didn't try to get rid of all the Vikings in Britain. Instead, he and Guthrum agreed the Vikings could stay in some of the kingdoms they had already taken over, like East Anglia and Northumbria. They also agreed that Guthrum would become a Christian.

Was this clever? Well, it meant ordinary people all over Britain had a few years of peace. And to become a Christian, Guthrum had to be baptised, which meant he needed a godfather. Alfred became that godfather, which was a way of showing how he was now Guthrum's overlord. The Vikings saw *their* king looking up to the *Saxon* king.

Alfred also realised that asking ordinary men to fight in battles wasn't the best idea. Instead, he trained proper soldiers, and built forts for them all over the kingdoms he looked after. These forts were known as *burhs*.

He also made better boats. Viking ships had always been a bit longer and faster than Saxon ships. Not anymore. Alfred wanted his ships to be as powerful as the old Roman ones.

All this meant that, when Guthrum died and the Vikings began to get mean again, Alfred was ready. There were a number of battles towards the end of Alfred's reign, but eventually those Vikings gave up and decided to stay in East Anglia and Northumbria.

Alfred knew the Saxons didn't just need soldiers. They also needed clever people. And people get clever by learning. So Alfred set up schools – mainly for noble children, but some poorer children were allowed in too. They learned to read and write – two skills that Alfred used a lot himself.

ALFRED + BEDE = 'ENGLISH'

Alfred encouraged his nobles to read Bede's *Ecclesiastical History of the English People*. Remember, this was a book where an Angle in Northumbria described all the Germanic nations in Britain as if they were part of the same family. Alfred clearly liked this idea, and started using Angles to mean his own people too – even though they were Saxons.

Alfred himself never wrote the word 'England'. After his big battle with Guthrum, he didn't try to take over any other kingdoms in Britain. But by calling his people Angles instead of Saxons, he allowed the Angles living all over Britain to think of Saxons as their friends.

This had been Bede's idea, but Alfred helped it take off! Now the Anglo-Saxons thought of themselves as one family, which they called the *Angelcynn* – which means 'English people'.

In fact, even before Alfred died, he and his people were starting to call their language *Englisc* – just one letter away from the language this book is written in!

So from now on, we don't need to say whether people are Angles or Saxons. We can call them *English*.

KING OF...?

Whenever we meet a king in this book, we'll take a moment to find out what he called himself. This can give us a clue as to whether he *thought* he had made a country called England. We've already seen one example in our introduction: Alfred's grandfather, King Egbert, who ruled every Germanic kingdom in AD 830 but preferred to keep calling himself 'King of the West Saxons' – he clearly *didn't* think he'd made England.

Alfred also called himself 'King of the West Saxons', and sometimes just 'King of the Saxons'. But his friend Asser gave him a new title in his book of stories about Alfred: 'King of the Anglo-Saxons'. That title almost made it onto some of the coins produced in Alfred's kingdoms – but, perhaps because of the small space, it only came out as 'King of the Anglo'.

Since we know that Alfred started using the word 'Englisc', it may be something of a surprise that Alfred never called himself 'King of the Englisc'. But one of his friends *outside* of Britain called him something close: a French Archbishop called Fulco wrote a letter to Alfred and called him (in Latin) 'King of the English'.

So Alfred was never a king of England – but it's almost certain that England wouldn't have existed without him...

SUMMARY

When Alfred became king, he was one of the last Anglo-Saxon kings in Britain – and it looked like he wouldn't last long. But Alfred eventually helped the Anglo-Saxons take large parts of Britain back.

He also called the Anglo-Saxons 'English'. This was Bede's idea, but maybe Alfred liked it because he knew the Anglo-Saxons would do better if they worked together. Both facts and folklore suggest Alfred saw examples of this: be it to surprise the Vikings, build new fortresses... or bake some cakes!

AUTHOR'S SCORESHEET

POWER 8

POPULARITY 10

INFLUENCE ON WHAT CAME NEXT 8

MAKER OF ENGLAND? 8

YOUR SCORESHEET

POWER ☐

POPULARITY ☐

INFLUENCE ON WHAT CAME NEXT ☐

MAKER OF ENGLAND? ☐

ETHELFLED

In AD 886, the kingdom of Mercia was split between the Vikings and the English. These were mostly peaceful times, though occasionally some cheeky Vikings (not Guthrum, of course...) tried their luck at stealing some English treasures.

Alfred wanted to stay friends with Ethelred, who ruled the English side of Mercia. So when Alfred heard that Ethelred fancied his daughter, Alfred asked his daughter to marry Ethelred. She was delighted to.

Alfred's daughter was Princess Ethelfled.

A QUICK NOTE ON OLD ENGLISH NAMES

Since you're reading this book, you're probably already interested in history, and I wouldn't be surprised if you start looking in other books to find out more about these characters.

In case you do, here's a quick warning: their names aren't always spelled the same way! Old English had a letter we don't use today: æ.

It looks a bit like an a and e stuck together, doesn't it? It was used a lot by Alfred's family. In fact, Alfred's name was originally spelled 'Ælfred'.

However, because æ isn't on keyboards today, people don't tend to use it anymore. Instead, they swap it for a different letter.

But which one? A or E? Sometimes it's obvious. For example, there are still people called Alfred today – so it makes sense to use an A.

Names like Æthelflæd, though, are harder to work out. Neither Athelflad or Ethelfled are names you hear much nowadays.

I've chosen 'Ethelfled' because at least part of this name is still around today – I've met girls called Ethel. So, for names like hers, I'm going to spell them with an E – even when they are boys' names like Ethelstan and Ethelred.

But if you look for these names somewhere else, like the index of a history book, bear in mind you might need to spell them differently. For example, 'Athelflad' – or even 'Aethelflaed'!

FOLKLORE: THE WARRIOR PRINCESS

For Alfred, the marriage of Ethelred and Ethelfled was bittersweet – he now had a powerful new son-in-law, but his daughter would be moving away. The morning after the wedding, he said farewell to Ethelfled.

Watching, Ethelred smiled gently. 'Don't worry, Alfred. I'll look after her.'

Alfred raised an eyebrow. 'Actually, Ethelred, I won't be surprised if she looks after you! The amount of time she's practised sword-fighting with her brothers...'

A few hours later, Ethelred and Ethelfled were riding their horses along the valleys of Mercia. But they weren't riding together. In those days men rode with men, and women rode with women.

The hills on each side of them were covered in trees, so it was quite dark even though it was still daylight. They were close to the border with East Mercia, the land controlled by the Vikings. But the Vikings and the English were at peace now, thanks to Alfred, so they didn't have to worry about –

'**Get them!**'

Suddenly, Viking highwaymen jumped out from behind the trees. It was an ambush! They rushed at the Mercian guards, knocking two of them into the muddy track with sword holes in their chests.

Ethelred shouted to two of his guards: 'Protect the princess!'

From the corner of his eye, Ethelred saw those guards spur their horses back towards his new wife. Ethelred and his remaining guards slashed their swords at the attackers. But it was hard, as the Vikings had them surrounded. Most of Ethelred's men had their swords knocked out of their hands within the first minute. Soon, Ethelred and his men were holding up their hands in surrender to a circle of greedy Vikings.

The Viking leader sneered. 'Right you lot, hand over your treasures!'

Ethelred had no choice. He passed his satchel across.

As the Viking leader took it, he noticed Ethelred's face – and gasped. 'Hey, guys! It's Lord Ethelred himself! This is our lucky day! We just wanted to rob some rich Englishmen, but we've caught the richest man in Mercia! Well, let's see what treasures you have for us...'

As the Viking looked into Ethelred's bag, a voice cried, 'How's this for treasure?'

The Viking looked up – straight into the pointy end of a spear flying towards his face.

The other Vikings instantly lifted their swords – but their surprise attackers, charging on horses, were too fast for them. Within seconds, the Vikings were either lying on the track in puddles of blood, or sprinting away in horror.

Ethelred was pleased to be alive, but was also shocked by the surprise rescuers. They were all women, each one holding a spear or a sword in her hand – including their leader: Ethelfled.

Ethelfled beamed at her new husband. 'What's that you said about looking after me?'

IS IT TRUE?

No one really knows. The story isn't in any books from the time, so it was probably only told by word of mouth for many years.

But if people wanted to tell it again and again, they must have liked it. Since Ethelfled is the heroine, that probably means they liked her as well.

LADY OF THE MERCIANS

Folklore is really important for understanding Ethelfled, because the facts are a little confusing.

We know she was Alfred's daughter, and that she married Ethelred of Mercia. We also know she did a lot to make Mercia a strong country again, like building fortresses to guard against Vikings. We even know she led the first army to take back control of the city of Derby from the Vikings.

Or at least, we think we know all this. Because it also looks like Ethelfled and her brother Edward may have fallen out.

We'll meet Edward in the next chapter: he took over from Alfred in Wessex. Both Edward and Ethelfled asked writers to continue Alfred's *Anglo-Saxon Chronicle*. But Edward's version hardly mentions Ethelfled at all, and makes it look like Edward won all those battles against the Vikings on his own. Only Ethelfled's version tells us what she did – and that version is mostly lost.

(I say 'mostly' because some bits of it were copied into other books we *do* still have today. But Ethelfled's *Chronicle* itself has completely disappeared.)

Did Edward get rid of Ethelfled's *Chronicle* because he was jealous? Some historians think Edward wanted to become king of Mercia when Ethelfled died, so he destroyed her version of the *Chronicle* to stop people thinking Mercia didn't need him.

Of course, it's also possible that it was Ethelfled's *Chronicle* that was full of lies, to make her look better than she actually was. But the folklore suggests people liked her anyway – so would she need to lie?

When Ethelfled's husband got sick around AD 901, Ethelfled began acting like a queen. This was unusual in those times – women hardly ever got to be in charge! Perhaps this is another clue that people liked her (or the Mercians did, at least): they were happy for her to be one of the first powerful English women.

FOLKLORE: THE DEFENCE OF CHESTER

The city of Chester was in West Mercia, the English side – but some Vikings lived there too. They had come from Ireland after falling out with an Irish king. They asked Ethelfled very nicely if they could stay in Chester, and she agreed.

But in AD 902, some Vikings in East Mercia learned about the Irish Vikings in Chester – and got excited. If all the Vikings got together, maybe they could take over Chester! Even more Englishmen would bow to a Viking king...

A Viking army snuck into the forests just outside Chester, and sent spies into the city to call the Irish Vikings out. All the Vikings then met in the trees to plan an attack on Chester.

But some of the Irish Vikings actually quite liked Ethelfled for giving them a home – so they secretly returned to Chester to warn her.

When the Vikings arrived to attack, they were surprised to find the guards on a break, and the city gates wide open. This was going to be easy! They walked through the gates with a bit of a skip and a jump...

...straight into an ambush from the Chester guards! The Vikings ran for their lives. As they reached the edge of the forest, they heard the guards shouting, 'And don't come back!'

But the Vikings didn't give up that easily. They made a new plan: to spread out around the city and climb up the walls. Then they could drop down on the guards inside – putting the pointy ends of their swords first!

Back in Chester, the guards saw Vikings coming towards them on all sides, carrying ladders. It was obvious what they were going to try.

The commander rushed to Ethelfled with the news.

Ethelfled thought for a moment, then asked, 'Are they carrying shields?'

'No, ma'am,' replied the commander, 'just swords and ladders.'

Ethelfled smiled. 'In that case, order everyone in the city to bring their heaviest items of furniture to the city walls.'

A short while later, the Vikings were halfway up the sides of the city walls.

Suddenly the head of an English guard popped up over the wall and said, 'Have a seat!'

The Vikings below were puzzled for a moment – until they saw a heavy oak chair falling towards them!

Another guard looked over. 'Elbows off the table!' he cried, before dropping a table down to knock even more Vikings off their ladders.

Yet another guard looked over to ask, 'What's cooking?' Then he dropped a collection of pots and pans down on the Vikings below.

Surprised, bruised, and defeated again, the Vikings hastily retreated.

But the Vikings didn't give up that easily. They made a new plan: to send some Vikings with shields up the walls first, while the rest carried swords.

Back in Chester, the guards saw Vikings coming towards them on all sides, carrying ladders *and* shields. It was obvious what they were going to try.

The commander rushed to Ethelfled with the news.

Ethelfled thought for a moment, then asked, 'Do we have plenty of mead?'

Mead is a kind of wine made with honey instead of grapes. The commander scratched his head. 'Er, yes your ladyship. Should we invite them to a party?'

Ethelfled chuckled. 'No, silly. Begin by heating up a few pots of mead.'

A short while later, the Vikings were halfway up the sides of the city walls.

Suddenly the head of an English guard popped up over the edge of the wall and asked, 'Thirsty?'

The Vikings below were puzzled for a moment – until boiling mead poured down over their heads!

Of course, it wasn't easy to bat away hot liquid honey. It stuck to the shields, burning the hands of the Vikings holding them. And it ran round the outside to drip down onto the faces of the Vikings below. The intense pain made the Vikings let go of their ladders, and they crashed to the ground with heavy thuds.

Surprised, bruised, scalded and defeated again, the Vikings hastily retreated.

But the Vikings didn't give up that easily. They made a new plan: to cover their shields with leather. That would make them heatproof against boiling honey.

Back in Chester, the guards saw Vikings coming towards them on all sides, carrying ladders and shields covered in leather. It was obvious what they were going to try.

The commander rushed to Ethelfled with the news.

Ethelfled thought for a moment, then said, 'Find the beekeepers who make the mead.'

The commander shook his head. 'Your ladyship – they've protected themselves against boiling mead.'

But Ethelfled smiled again. 'We're not asking for mead this time.'

A short while later, the Vikings were halfway up the sides of the city walls.

Suddenly the head of an English guard popped up over the edge of the wall and said, 'This may sting a little...'

The Vikings below were puzzled for a moment – until *beehives* were thrown over the walls!

The hives smashed on the Viking shields – and swarms of bees flew out. Angry bees will always attack the nearest creatures – which, in this case, were Vikings on ladders.

Seconds later the Vikings crashed to the ground again, their skin swelling and itching from the stings of hundreds of bees.

Surprised, bruised, scalded, stung, and defeated again, the Vikings hastily retreated.

And this time, when they met in the forest, the Vikings decided to leave Chester alone.

Back inside those city walls, the people of Chester held a huge celebration in honour of their wise queen Ethelfled.

IS IT TRUE?

I hope so! I love the idea of the Vikings coming back again and again, but getting beaten with a new and clever idea each time – don't you?

Being such fun might explain why this story was passed around for so long. But sadly we don't know for sure when the story was first told, let alone if it's true.

We do know there *was* an attack on Chester, by Vikings from both East Mercia and Ireland. Some old books also say that Ethelfled protected Chester with the help of some Irish Vikings.

Once again, this story tells us that people thought Ethelfled was a good and clever queen.

SUMMARY

Ethelfled is one of the trickiest characters in this book. Folklore tells us she was as clever as her father Alfred, and shared his hope that all people would get along – even allowing Irish Vikings to come and live in Chester. So you could say she helped make England by putting unity above the desire to fight.

On the other hand, Ethelfled was only a heroine for *some* of the English: those living in Mercia. Perhaps this encouraged Mercians to feel different to the English in other parts of Britain – and that may have kept the kingdoms apart for longer. Although our next character became overlord of Mercia, the Mercians chose their own king again just fifty years later (see **'Edwy the Fair'**).

Did the Mercians revolt because Ethelfled made them feel like Mercia was the best English kingdom? If so, Ethelfled was probably the *opposite* of an England-maker...

AUTHOR'S SCORESHEET

POWER | 7
POPULARITY | 8
INFLUENCE ON WHAT CAME NEXT | 6
MAKER OF ENGLAND? | 5

YOUR SCORESHEET

POWER

POPULARITY

INFLUENCE ON WHAT CAME NEXT

MAKER OF ENGLAND?

EDWARD THE ELDER

When Alfred died in AD 899, his son Edward became king of Wessex. But while Alfred preferred making peace with Vikings and making his kingdom stronger, Edward wanted to *use* that strength – to get rid of all the Viking kings in Britain.

Edward liked Alfred's idea that all the Germanic nations in Britain were English. Since there were English people ruled by Vikings in kingdoms like East Anglia and Northumbria, a lot of historians think Edward attacked those Vikings to rescue the English.

But Edward also took over Mercia when his sister Ethelfled died – and, as we've seen, the Mercians didn't think they needed rescuing...

HOW MANY EDS?

If you check the contents page, you'll see that there are two King Edwards in this book. You'll also meet two *other* King Edwards before the end of this book. So why aren't they called Edward I, II, III, etc.?

Remember: William the Conqueror made everyone think he was the first important king of England for a while. So the first Edward *after* William became King Edward I – and that wasn't until 1272.

Instead, the Edwards *before* William each have special names to help us tell them apart. *This* Edward is called 'the Elder' for one simple reason: he was older than the others!

EDWARD THE BORING

Being called 'Edward the Elder' does tell us something though: the English had nothing special to say about him.

When you look at the facts, this may seem surprising. Edward achieved a lot as king. For instance, he helped his sister defend Wessex and Mercia from the Vikings, and cleared Viking rulers out of nearly every other kingdom in Britain except Northumbria. Even some Scots and Welsh ended up calling him overlord.

But despite all this, there's not one piece of folklore about him. So, was he really a hero rescuing the English all over Britain? Or was he actually a bit, well, boring?

Perhaps there's a clue in one of the facts: a battle between Edward's soldiers and the Vikings at a place called the Holme in East Anglia, around AD 902.

Ethelwold, Edward's cousin, had joined forces with the Vikings to try and become king all over Britain. He asked the Vikings in East Anglia to help him attack Mercia.

While they were gone, though, Edward took his army to attack the *peasants* in East Anglia

– probably setting fire to their farms and houses like William the Conqueror did later. He did this so Ethelwold's Viking army would leave Mercia alone and come back home.

The plan worked. However, when Edward found out that the East Anglian Vikings were coming home, bringing Ethelwold with them, he ordered his men to retreat instead of staying to fight. We don't know why. Was he scared? Did he think his army would fight better from their homes in Kent and Wessex? Or did he just not want to fight his cousin?

But the soldiers from Kent decided they wouldn't do as they were told. They stayed in East Anglia to fight the Vikings anyway – and won!

Well, kind of. The records actually say the Vikings won. But they also say all the Viking leaders in that battle were killed – including Ethelwold. So the Vikings probably didn't feel too happy!

In the previous chapter, we mentioned how Edward and Ethelfled both asked writers to keep Alfred's *Anglo-Saxon Chronicle* up to date – but Edward's version ended up being different to Ethelfled's version. Edward's made him look like the hero of all the English.

Is that why Edward's *Chronicle* says that the soldiers of Kent lost, even though they defeated the Viking leaders? Perhaps Edward didn't want to admit that the English could win without him? After all, Edward doesn't look like a good king if his soldiers make decisions without him and then go on to win.

The fact that the English in Kent disobeyed Edward in the first place also tells us that they didn't care about him as much as the Mercians cared about Ethelfled.

KING OF...?

For a while, Edward was 'King of the West Saxons'. He seems to have liked his father's idea of calling himself 'King of the Anglo-Saxons', though, and eventually started using this himself – but for some reason this doesn't seem to have made it onto his coins. The ones we've found so far only seem to call him 'King' – and that's it!

SUMMARY

Edward can't have been a *bad* king. There aren't any stories about him being terrible. But there aren't any stories about him being great either. It's true that Edward brought more of the English kingdoms together. But maybe those other kings accepted Edward as overlord because they were more afraid of English *soldiers* than the English *king*?

AUTHOR'S SCORESHEET

POWER | 7

POPULARITY | 4

INFLUENCE ON WHAT CAME NEXT | 5

MAKER OF ENGLAND? | 4

YOUR SCORESHEET

POWER | ☐

POPULARITY | ☐

INFLUENCE ON WHAT CAME NEXT | ☐

MAKER OF ENGLAND? | ☐

ELFWEARD

Some old books suggest that Edward's *second* oldest son, Elfweard, became king next.

For sixteen days or so.

So it's probably not surprising that there isn't much folklore *or* fact about him! All the old books tell different stories. The *Anglo-Saxon Chronicle* says he died sixteen days after Edward. A list of kings made later says Elfweard lived for twenty-eight days, and was definitely a king. Some old books say he was king of Wessex, and a few historians think this means he was *only* king of Wessex – he didn't get to be overlord of other kingdoms like his father. And still other old books don't mention Elfweard at all!

Why bother mentioning him then? Well, he is proof of one thing: we can't always trust old books to give us facts!

ETHELSTAN

Ethelstan was Edward's oldest son, so was ready to become king when Edward died in AD 924. However, old books tell us that he wasn't given the crown until one year later. Was that because Elfweard was king first? Or because the English didn't want Ethelstan to be king, and were trying to choose someone else?

By the time Ethelstan died, though, some people were calling him 'King of All Britain'. All the English, Scottish, Welsh, and Vikings on the island accepted him as their overlord. Even some Irish kings

bowed to him! So, some historians today call Ethelstan 'the first king of England'.

But was he?

FOLKLORE: EVERYONE'S FAVOURITE PRINCE

One old book tells how, as a little boy, Ethelstan looked after his grandfather, Alfred the Great. When Alfred got poorly in his old age, Ethelstan wiped the sweat away from his forehead. To reward his favourite grandson, Alfred wrote a will saying that Ethelstan *had* to be the next king of Wessex after Edward.

Shortly after Alfred died, Ethelstan went to stay with his aunt Ethelfled in Mercia. Together they practised sword fighting, and discussed battle strategies every day.

Ethelfled had a daughter called Elfwynn. This princess should have become queen of Mercia after Ethelfled died. But instead, because Ethelfled liked Ethelstan so much, she wrote in her will that Ethelstan should be the next ruler of Mercia – and Elfwynn had to become a nun.

IS IT TRUE?

Well, this is the same old book that tells us Elfweard never became king – which may or may not be true. The wills of Alfred and Ethelfled don't exist anymore, so we can't check.

Ethelstan was about five years old when Alfred died, so he *could* have looked after his grandfather. And other books tell us Ethelstan joined Ethelfled's army in fights against the Vikings – so nephew and aunt probably did get on quite well together.

Whatever the truth, folklore has already told us that Alfred and Ethelfled were popular. Since both of them are said to have really liked Ethelstan, perhaps that shows us *people* liked Ethelstan too?

KING OF ALL THE ENGLISH

Edward became overlord for most kingdoms in Britain. But Ethelstan wanted to do better than that. He wanted to be the overlord *everywhere* in Britain! He couldn't do that while there was still a Viking king in Northumbria.

It was around AD 927 that Ethelstan got rid of the last Viking king in Northumbria (for now, at least). But he didn't stop there. He kept going north, fighting the Scots until *they* called him overlord.

However, the Scots didn't like that much. They found some Vikings to help, and invaded Northumbria.

Ethelstan didn't rush to fight them. He took his time gathering a large English army, then marched north...

FOLKLORE: BLESSED FOR SUCCESS

As Ethelstan rode his horse at the head of his army, he heard his soldiers whispering behind him.

'There's loads of them! We'll be outnumbered!'

'I've heard Vikings from Ireland have come to help them.'

'We don't stand a chance!'

Ethelstan knew they were probably right. There was only one thing to do.

He halted his horse, and ordered his entire army to take a new route – through a village called Beverley in East Mercia.

Ethelstan's commander blinked. 'But sir, we're close to the west coast of Britain right now – Beverley is near the east coast. Your soldiers will get tired!'

Ethelstan just shrugged. 'We're going there first. That's an order.'

*

It took half a day to reach Beverley. By the time they got there, all the soldiers wanted to sleep.

But Ethelstan had other ideas. He took his soldiers to the nearby monastery, where there was a shrine to a Christian saint called John, and told them, 'St John was a friend of Bede, who inspired my grandfather Alfred to unite Britain under one God. So pray to St John, and he'll be on our side when we fight the non-Christian Scots and Vikings tomorrow!'

Whether the soldiers believed him or not, Ethelstan certainly prayed as hard as *he* could. He even gave gifts to the monks looking after St John's shrine, so the monastery shone with riches.

That night, as Ethelstan's army camped outside of Beverley, Ethelstan lay awake in his sheepskin rugs, worrying about the battle to come.

Suddenly his tent was filled with a dazzling light, and a man dressed in white floated in front of him.

'Ethelstan, why are you worried? Remember: I'll be with you.'

Ethelstan had seen the floating man's face before, on one of the stained-glass windows at Beverley monastery: it was St John himself!

IS IT TRUE?

This story was first written down by a priest living about 200 years later, so we don't know for sure that Ethelstan visited Beverley with his army.

We do know, though, that Ethelstan's army *did* win the fight that came next, known as the Battle of Brunanburh. And afterwards, every king in Britain called Ethelstan their overlord.

KING OF ALL BRITAIN?

Or did they?

Well, that's what most of the old books say. But we don't just find facts in books. Sometimes we can find facts through other objects, too.

Coins are a good way to discover facts about kings. Just like British coins today, medieval coins carried the name of whoever was in charge. And historians have certainly found coins calling Ethelstan the 'King of All Britain'.

The thing is, these coins weren't made *everywhere*. In Mercia, for example, the coins called Ethelstan 'King of the *Saxons*'. They weren't even calling him king of the *English*, like his father and grandfather!

The coins in East Anglia or Northumbria didn't call Ethelstan 'King of All Britain' either – so maybe the Vikings living there weren't happy calling Ethelstan their overlord?

Other written records, though, make it look like Ethelstan had a lot of power. Ethelstan spent a lot of time in Wessex, but the rulers of other kingdoms visited him regularly. If they were happy to make those journeys, they must have respected Ethelstan.

Whether we look at coins, books, or anything else, it seems the English nation couldn't agree as to whether they liked him or not. Sure, there may have been stories of him speaking with saints – but there were also tales of him being rather mean...

FOLKLORE: THE SHAMEFUL PRINCE

Ethelstan had lots of brothers – and that meant there were lots of potential kings living around him. So it was especially tricky for Ethelstan if one brother became more popular than him...

That's what happened with Prince Edwin. He had stayed in Wessex while Ethelstan went to help Ethelfled in Mercia. Edwin made friends with many Wessex nobles. He used to joke that, if he ever got to be king, he would do whatever they wanted.

When Ethelstan won the Battle of Brunanburh, though, these nobles believed God must be on Ethelstan's side. Now they wanted to be *Ethelstan's* best friends.

But the nobles knew that Ethelstan thought Wessex didn't like him. So they concocted a wicked plan to change his mind...

The next time they met Ethelstan, the nobles told him, 'Your Majesty, Edwin is plotting against you! He's asked soldiers to pull out your eyes – because everyone knows a blind man can't be king. Your brother wants to be king instead of you!'

Ethelstan was outraged. He immediately ordered his guards to drag Edwin to the beach.

Edwin pleaded with his brother, and brought along a friend who pleaded for him too. Remember: in English law, that could help you win an argument.

But Ethelstan refused to change his mind, and instead forced Edwin into a leaky boat – with the friend, too!

The boat had no oars, sail, food or water. Ethelstan's guards pushed it out to sea – much to the delight of those Wessex nobles.

Of course, it wasn't long before the boat sank, taking Edwin and his friend with it. Whether Ethelstan ever discovered the treachery of the nobles, we may never know...

IS IT TRUE?

Possibly. The *Anglo-Saxon Chronicle* only tells us that Edwin drowned at sea (but remember, the *Chronicle* was written by friends of the king).

Another old book says Edwin was actually travelling to do a job for Ethelstan when his boat sank in an accident. The story I've shared here wasn't written down until about 200 years later, though it was collected by two different medieval historians.

It does give us a clue about what some people thought of Ethelstan though: he could be jealous, quick-tempered, and gullible.

KING OF...?

As we've already mentioned, Ethelstan used different titles in different parts of Britain – so we can't be sure exactly how powerful Ethelstan really was.

There is one more title that Ethelstan began using, though – one that people in other countries had used for his grandfather Alfred: 'King of the English'. So Ethelstan must have thought he ruled all the *English* people in Britain, at least. But did all the English agree?

SUMMARY

We can't be sure exactly how powerful Ethelstan really was. Some historians think he was right to call himself 'King of All Britain' – after all, every other ruler in Britain visited him regularly. They wouldn't have bothered if they didn't respect him!

But we also know that some kingdoms didn't like calling Ethelstan their king or overlord. And though folklore tells us some people thought Ethelstan had Alfred, Ethelfled, and God on his side, it also tells us some people thought Ethelstan could be easily tricked.

All-in-all, Ethelstan doesn't seem to have completely united the *people* across the English kingdoms, even if he did rule all the kingdoms that would eventually become England. And, as we'll see, this wasn't the last time those kingdoms had separate kings either...

AUTHOR'S SCORESHEET

POWER [9]

POPULARITY [7]

INFLUENCE ON WHAT CAME NEXT [7]

MAKER OF ENGLAND? [7]

YOUR SCORESHEET

POWER [ ]

POPULARITY [ ]

INFLUENCE ON WHAT CAME NEXT [ ]

MAKER OF ENGLAND? [ ]

EDMUND

Ethelstan didn't have any children. Fortunately for Alfred's family, though, Ethelstan had several brothers. The next eldest was Edmund.

WHO GETS TO BE THE NEXT KING?

In those days, the king's oldest son became the next king. If there weren't any sons, the crown went to the king's next eldest brother. Remember: that's how Alfred got to be king – this was the English way.

But it wasn't the *Viking* way. When a Viking leader died, the top Viking warriors met to decide the next one. Sometimes they chose the last leader's son, but not always.

When Ethelstan died in AD 939, the Vikings in Northumbria decided they didn't want Edmund as their king. Instead, they chose a Viking called Olaf.

Olaf wasn't satisfied with ruling Northumbria alone. He quickly helped the Vikings reconquer several English lands that used to be ruled by Vikings – including parts of Mercia.

Edmund managed to get the Viking leaders out of Mercia again – but he never got to be quite as powerful as his dad or older brother.

FOLKLORE: THE GOLDEN APPLE

After a battle, winners normally took treasures from the losers. So, after beating the Vikings in Mercia, Edmund took several Viking treasures back to Wessex.

Once at home, Edmund sat in his private chamber and went through these trinkets. There were many precious things: patterned plates, jewelled axes, pretty paintings... All would make great decorations for his fortress.

But one treasure was more unusual: an apple made entirely of gold. Edmund found these words written on the apple:

To be blessed by all the Heavenly host,
Give this fruit to whom you love the most.

Edmund thought a blessing from all the Heavenly host could be useful. He thought hard: who did he love the most? His eldest son Edwy? His youngest son Edgar? His wife Elfgifu?

Just then, Edmund's dog barked, and the king smiled. That happy canine face always cheered Edmund up.

'You want to play, boy?' Edmund was about to reach for his pet's favourite ball, when he realised he was still holding the golden apple. So he smiled and said, 'You know what, boy? You're always at my side in times of joy, sorrow, war, and peace. I think I love *you* the most. So... here!'

As Edmund threw the apple for his dog, however, the door to his chamber opened. Elfgifu, Edmund's wife, stepped inside just as the apple flew through the air – and she caught it.

Before Edmund could say anything, Elfgifu rushed over and gave him a huge hug. 'Oh,

Edmund, I love it – it's beautiful! I *knew* you'd bring me something expensive back from Mercia. I'll treasure this, I really will!'

With that, Elfgifu rushed out of his room, straight to her own room. There she sat and admired the golden apple in closer detail. As she did, she found the words:

> *To be blessed by all the Heavenly host,*
> *Give this fruit to whom you love the most.*

Elfgifu thought a blessing from all the Heavenly host could be useful. She thought hard: who did she love the most?

It didn't take her long to figure it out. For a long time, Elfgifu had fancied the commander of Edmund's army. She went to see him straight away.

The commander was leaving the dining hall when Elfgifu found him. She blushed a little as she went over to him, holding out the apple. 'A special reward. For all your hard work in Mercia.'

Before the commander could say thank you, Elfgifu shyly turned and skipped away. The commander looked down at his prize – and saw the words:

To be blessed by all the Heavenly host,
Give this fruit to whom you love the most.

The commander thought a blessing from all the Heavenly host could be useful. And he knew *exactly* who he loved the most.

He went straight back into the dining hall. His girlfriend, one of the maids, was cleaning the tables.

The commander kissed her cheek, and handed her the apple. She immediately kissed him back – she was over the moon! No one had ever given her such an expensive present!

The commander went back to work, and the maid looked down at the golden apple. She saw the words...

...but she couldn't read. So she popped the apple into the pouch of her pinny, and finished her cleaning.

That evening, the maid had to babysit young prince Edgar. She took him into the gardens to play. They sat facing each other, then the maid took the golden apple from her apron and rolled it to him. Edgar squealed in delight, then rolled it back to her.

They played this game for several minutes, until Edgar suddenly gave a wide yawn. The maid sat beside him, and cuddled him into her lap.

Edgar soon fell asleep. Watching him, the maid felt drowsy too. She tried to stay awake, but eventually she slipped into a dream.

The golden apple lay on the grass by the maid's feet... until along came a dog, out for its evening walk. The animal bounced over to the apple, and happily picked it up in his jaws. Then he dashed back to his owner, who was out walking with him.

'What have you got there, boy?'

King Edmund held out his hands, and the dog gave him the golden apple.

Edmund smiled, and patted his pet. 'My boy, you are the most blessed dog who ever lived.'

IS IT TRUE?

This lovely tale is told all over Britain – but the king isn't always Edmund. Sometimes the king is Scottish, and sometimes the king doesn't have any name at all.

So was it a true story about Edmund that then changed to be about other kings? Was it a true story about another king that got changed to be about Edmund? Or was it just completely made up, and people chose whoever they liked to be the king in the story?

Whatever the answer (and we'll never know for sure), what does it tell us that people put Edmund in this story? Do you see a thoughtful king, who cared about those who showed him loyalty? Or a gullible man, who wasn't even in love with his wife?

THE DEATH OF EDMUND

Edmund was only king for seven years. According to some old books, he was at a party when he noticed that a famous thief called Liofa had snuck into the hall.

Edmund didn't bother to summon the guards – he went right over to arrest Liofa himself. But Liofa slashed at the king with a knife. Guards rushed over as soon as they noticed, but it was too late. Edmund lay dead on the floor.

Remember: just because this story was written down doesn't mean it's true. Liofa may actually have been an assassin sent to kill the king, but one of Edmund's friends wanted to make it sound like Edmund died a hero.

KING OF...?

Like his brother and his grandfather, Edmund would call himself 'King of the Anglo-Saxons' or 'King of the English'. Sometimes he would call himself both on the same piece of paper.

He didn't use Ethelstan's title of 'King of All Britain' – perhaps because the number of kingdoms he ruled at the end of his reign was smaller than at the start. But one of his titles shows that he at least *tried* to rule over more people than just the English: he called himself 'King of the English *and the surrounding nations*'.

SUMMARY

Edmund certainly didn't help make England. The number of kingdoms he ruled was smaller at the end of his reign than the start.

However, being the hero of a folk tale found all over Britain might show that people could move about easily between Edmund's kingdoms, carrying stories with them. Maybe this happened because the kingdoms were slowly merging into one?

AUTHOR'S SCORESHEET

POWER 7

POPULARITY 7

INFLUENCE ON WHAT CAME NEXT 4

MAKER OF ENGLAND? 4

YOUR SCORESHEET

POWER

POPULARITY

INFLUENCE ON WHAT CAME NEXT

MAKER OF ENGLAND?

EADRED

Thanks to Liofa, Edmund died in AD 946 when his son was only about six years old – not old enough to be king. So Eadred, Ethelstan's next oldest brother, became king instead.

Meanwhile, the Vikings in Northumbria had chosen a leader they were sure would scare the English away: *Eric Bloodaxe.*

So, soon after becoming king, Eadred took an army to Northumbria. But he didn't fight Bloodaxe. Instead, he burned some of the farms and homes

in Northumbria, and told the people he would burn even more unless they got rid of Bloodaxe themselves. The Northumbrians believed him, and soon told Bloodaxe to leave. They chose another man called Olaf instead – for about three years. Then they brought Bloodaxe back. So, once again, Eadred went to Northumbria with his army to tell them – again – to get rid of Bloodaxe.

It wasn't so fast the second time, but Bloodaxe did eventually leave – and the Northumbrians finally allowed Eadred to be their king.

Eadred was king for nine years. One old book says he died of a disease that made it hard for him to chew his food – so he was always sucking on things like bones of chicken, often dribbling. It made him smell disgusting too.

KING OF...?

Eadred didn't call himself 'King of All Britain', like his brother Ethelstan. Instead, he mostly stuck with Edmund's idea of being called 'King of the English and the surrounding nations' – though sometimes he went for 'King of the English, Northumbrians, Pagans and Britons'...!

Why the fancy long title? Possibly because it made him look stronger! But it also proves that Eadred hadn't stuck all the kingdoms together to make just one – he at least thought Northumbria was a separate country.

SUMMARY

Eadred's reign was almost exactly the reverse of Edmund's. By the time Eadred died, the Northumbrians had allowed him to be their king. In fact, they didn't choose a Viking king again for a very long time.

So Eadred must have done something right. We don't have any folklore to let us know what people thought of Eadred, but the facts seem to suggest he was a powerful king – if a bit of a smelly one.

AUTHOR'S SCORESHEET

POWER `8`

POPULARITY `6`

INFLUENCE ON WHAT CAME NEXT `7`

MAKER OF ENGLAND? `6`

YOUR SCORESHEET

POWER ☐

POPULARITY ☐

INFLUENCE ON WHAT CAME NEXT ☐

MAKER OF ENGLAND? ☐

EDWY THE FAIR

By the time Eadred died in AD 955, Edmund's son Edwy had turned fifteen. He probably had lovely blond hair, which was why he got called 'the Fair'.

FOLKLORE: EDWY AND ELFGIFU

Like all English princes, Edwy was taught by some of the best monks in the land. But Edwy found it difficult to concentrate in class. He was much more interested in staring at Elfgifu, the pretty girl who shared lessons with him.

When Edwy heard that his uncle had died, he was of course sad – for a few minutes at least. But it wasn't long before he realised that, now he was king, he would need a queen…

On Edwy's coronation day, a huge feast was held in Wessex to celebrate. But the question on everybody's lips was, *Where is the king?*

Edwy was knocking on the door of Elfgifu's bedroom. He knew exactly what he wanted to say – but he also knew that, if he saw Elfgifu's beautiful face, he might get so nervous that he'd forget everything. So as the door opened, he closed his eyes and said, 'My darling. Now I'm king, I've decided: I want you to be my queen!'

'Oh, Edwy!'

Edwy smiled at how happy the voice sounded – then frowned. The voice sounded older than Elfgifu. He opened his eyes just in time to see *Ethelgifu*, Elfgifu's mum, reaching out to give him a huge hug.

'Wait!' he cried. 'I'm very sorry, Ethelgifu – I meant your daughter!'

Elfgifu was also in the room, and now stepped forward. She grabbed Edwy's arm and yanked him into a huge hug herself. 'Oh, Edwy!'

But Ethelgifu wasn't prepared to lose her chance to be queen that quickly. She snatched Edwy back into *her* embrace.

Elfgifu wasn't ready to give up either. She ran at her mother to push her out of the way, then threw her arms back around Edwy.

This went on for a few minutes. Edwy could have stopped it at any moment. But he was enjoying having two women fighting over him!

Suddenly a gasp came from the doorway – and all three turned to see Bishop Dunstan staring at them.

When he finally spoke, Dunstan's voice was firm. 'Your Majesty! That is *not* how a king should behave!'

The bishop then grabbed Edwy's arm and marched him back to the feast like a naughty teenager.

Edwy's face was bright red. Instead of eating, he watched Dunstan whispering to other people in the room. He knew everybody was talking about what had been going on in Elfgifu's room. He suddenly stood up and slammed the table.

The room went quiet.

Edwy glared at a servant. 'You! Tell me what's being said about me!'

The servant looked around the room, stunned and helpless.

Edwy scowled. 'Man, I am your king! Tell me the truth!'

The man lowered his head. 'They said Bishop Dunstan found you with a couple of strumpets, your Majesty...'

'What?!'

Edwy whirled to face Dunstan. The bishop now looked less confident. Edwy wasn't an ordinary teenage prince anymore – he was *king*.

Edwy pointed at him. 'You, bishop, are hereby sentenced to exile! How dare you call our future queen a strumpet! Get out of my sight before I think of a worse punishment for you!'

Dunstan left the room as quickly as he could.

*

Dunstan hid in France – but he still had friends in Wessex.

Those friends discovered that Elfgifu was actually one of Edwy's cousins. This meant they

could convince other people that Edwy and Elfgifu had to get a divorce. Even though he was king, Edwy couldn't do anything with all his subjects against him. So he just had to watch as Elfgifu was taken, put on a boat, and sent away.

No one really knows what happened to Elfgifu next. Some say Dunstan's friends killed her. Others say she went to Mercia, where Edwy's brother Edgar took pity on her – and let her live there in secret for the rest of her life.

But Edwy never saw her again. His heart broke – and, just four years later, he died.

IS IT TRUE?

All old books, including the *Anglo-Saxon Chronicle*, agree that Edwy and Dunstan had an argument. Some don't tell us why, though. It could have been because Dunstan caught Edwy with Elfgifu and her mum, but that could also be a nasty piece of gossip made up by Dunstan's friends to make Edwy look bad.

But Edwy did marry Elfgifu – and they were then forced to divorce, with Elfgifu being sent away.

Dunstan's friends also tried making Edwy's younger brother Edgar king. This wasn't easy in Wessex. People living there wanted to stick to the rule that the eldest prince became the next king, and that was still Edwy.

But people in other kingdoms *did* agree with Dunstan's friends – especially Mercians, who seemed eager to have a king of their own again. It looked like there would be a war between the English kingdoms unless Edwy did something soon.

In the end, to keep the peace, Edwy agreed to let Edgar rule the kingdoms in the north (including Mercia), while he remained king of Wessex and Kent in the south.

KING OF...?

For a while, it seems like Edwy tried to keep the title 'King of the English and the surrounding nations' – but, before long, he found himself stuck with just 'King of the English'.

SUMMARY

Edwy doesn't look like an England-maker. But his story is important, since it shows how the English kingdoms were still quite separate – even though many of them had been ruled together by English kings since Edward the Elder.

Whether or not the folklore about Edwy and Elfgifu is true, it certainly shows that people thought Edwy wasn't a very powerful king.

AUTHOR'S SCORESHEET

POWER [3]

POPULARITY [3]

INFLUENCE ON WHAT CAME NEXT [4]

MAKER OF ENGLAND? [1]

YOUR SCORESHEET

POWER ☐

POPULARITY ☐

INFLUENCE ON WHAT CAME NEXT ☐

MAKER OF ENGLAND? ☐

A BRIEF BREAK FROM BRITAIN

Let's leave Britain for a while, because something interesting happened on the other side of the North Sea that might hold a clue about where England came from...

Remember how there were different tribes of Vikings? One tribe was the *Danes*. These Vikings came from an area called *Jutland*, which sticks out from the north of Germany. Like Britain, Jutland was made up of several kingdoms, each ruled by a different Danish king.

But around AD 958, a man called Harald Bluetooth became king of all the Danish kingdoms. In celebration, Harald carved a memorial called a *Jelling stone*. The runes on the stone said:

Notice how Harald calls his land *Denmark*? It's still called that today. It seems Harald was the first king to unite the Danish kingdoms under one name.

So, while the English kings kept their kingdoms separate, a Danish king preferred to stick his smaller kingdoms together.

What could happen, then, if a Danish king controlled all the *English* kingdoms?

We'll have a chance to find out soon. But first, back to Britain...

EDGAR THE PEACEFUL

Edgar became king of Mercia and the other northern kingdoms to stop people fighting over whether Edwy should be king. But after Edwy died in AD 959, Edgar became king of Wessex and Kent too.

Dunstan returned from France to put the crown on Edgar's head, and made Edgar promise in public to try ensuring all his people lived in peace – a promise that every king and queen has copied since.

ALMOST ENGLAND

Edgar didn't give all the kingdoms a single name. But he *did* rule nearly every kingdom the same way.

For example, he made sure people in every kingdom used the same measurements for weight (if you've ever had to work out the difference between kilograms and stones, you'll understand how useful this was!). He also divided each kingdom into *shires*, to make them easier to rule. Many of these shires still exist today, such as Yorkshire, Cambridgeshire and Worcestershire.

So while the kingdoms weren't yet stuck together under one name, they began to share laws, taxes and coins.

Hardly any battles took place in Britain during Edgar's long reign, which is why he's called 'the Peaceful'. But Edgar himself may not have been a peaceful man...

FOLKLORE: ELFTHRYTH'S SUITORS

Edgar needed a queen. He already had several girlfriends, but he couldn't marry any of them: they weren't beautiful enough. Being the most powerful man in Britain, Edgar wanted to marry the most beautiful woman!

He sent spies to find the best-looking woman in Britain. When they came back, they all had the same answer: Elfthryth of Wessex.

Edgar didn't go to meet Elfthryth himself. He was the king – people had to come to *him*. Instead, he spoke to one of his most trusted nobles: 'Ethelwald. Go to Wessex and find this Elfthryth. If she really is as beautiful as everyone says she is, bring her to marry me.'

Elfthryth's home was near a forest in West Wessex. Once there, Ethelwald knocked on the door.

As Elfthryth opened the door, Ethelwald's heart seemed to pump pins and needles all around his body. He knew he should tell her that Edgar wanted to marry her – but instead, he found himself saying he was a lost traveller. He didn't mention Edgar at all.

Elfthryth was curious about this mystery guest. She knew from Ethelwald's clothes that he must be very rich. Her heart didn't skip any beats for Ethelwald, but her mind got a bit dizzy thinking about how rich he was. Plus it was obvious Ethelwald fancied her: he kept looking at her with wide, smiling, hopeful eyes.

So she let him take her for rides on his horse, and meals at the local taverns. Soon, Ethelwald asked her to marry him, and Elfthryth couldn't help but smile.

And of course she said, 'Yes.'

Now Ethelwald knew he would be in trouble if Edgar ever learned what had happened. So, after their wedding, Ethelwald travelled alone to visit the king, and told him all the spies were wrong: Elfthryth was really ugly. Edgar thanked Ethelwald for saving him from marrying her, and rewarded Ethelwald with plenty of riches.

Life continued happily for a while – until Edgar wondered why Ethelwald kept travelling to West Wessex instead of his home in East Anglia.

When Edgar asked about it, Ethelwald panicked. He blurted out, 'I got married! I now live there with my wife.'

Edgar raised his eyebrows. 'Why didn't you say? I'm happy for you, my friend! I shall journey to meet your new wife.'

Ethelwald was in a fix now. He couldn't refuse the king without looking suspicious. But if Edgar saw how beautiful Elfthryth was, Ethelwald would surely be punished severely for lying. So he told Edgar he just needed to tidy up his house, then sped home.

Elfthryth was worried when her husband returned looking terrified. Ethelwald quickly explained: 'I was supposed to get you to marry the king, but we fell in love instead. Now he's coming here, so we must hide your beauty!'

Elfthryth nodded, and agreed to cover herself in dirt to look as ugly as possible.

Secretly, though, Elfthryth was *furious*! She hadn't fallen in love with Ethelwald – she just liked his money. But being a queen was worth far more than any money! How dare Ethelwald steal her chance of power?

The next day, Edgar arrived with his guards. Ethelwald met him in the courtyard, then called Elfthryth.

Instead of coming out with dirt on her face, Elfthryth wore her best dress, her best wimple, and her best make-up. Immediately, Edgar realised he was looking at the gorgeous Elfthryth everyone had told him about. His tummy felt funny – he wanted this woman to be his queen.

For now, though, Edgar politely joined Ethelwald and Elfthryth for dinner. Elfthryth laughed at all Edgar's jokes. Edgar couldn't take his eyes off her.

Ethelwald felt his cheeks burning – what would be his punishment for lying?

But it seemed Ethelwald didn't have to worry. Edgar said goodnight without looking angry. Then, the following morning, Edgar asked Ethelwald to show him the best place to hunt nearby. It seemed everything was fine between them – Ethelwald and Edgar had often hunted together as young men.

Alas, on that hunt, an arrow from one of Edgar's men 'accidentally' hit Ethelwald's back. Edgar had to tell Elfthryth the sad news that her husband was dead.

Of course, Elfthryth cried – it would have looked strange if she didn't. But when Edgar offered to cheer her up by making her a queen, Elfthryth couldn't help but smile.

And of course she said, 'Yes.'

IS IT TRUE?

This is another tale first written down by William of Malmesbury, who was the first to write down 'Alfred the Minstrel'.

There are other old books that say Elfthryth married Edgar after her first husband Ethelwald died – but those don't mention Ethelwald hiding Elfthryth from Edgar, nor Edgar ordering his men to kill Ethelwald during a hunt.

This tale may have been popular even before William recorded it, though. It doesn't make Elfthryth look like a nice person, does it – and after Edgar died, other nasty rumours spread about Elfthryth (see the next chapter).

It *is* true that Edgar had lots of girlfriends before marrying Elfthryth, though – including a nun!

KING OF...?

It seems Edgar tried lots of different titles! He was 'King of the English and the surrounding nations' like his father and uncles; like Eadred, he tried a long and fancy title with 'King of the Mercians and Northumbrians and Britons'; and he even tried matching Ethelstan by calling himself 'Ruler of the Whole of Britain'!

But he still didn't choose 'King of England'...

SUMMARY

Because he didn't have to worry about fighting any other English or Viking kings, Edgar enjoyed sixteen years of nothing but hunting, feasting and lots of girlfriends. But he also made some very important changes to the English kingdoms that maybe helped them stick together later. Things like sharing coins, measurements, laws, etc.

So why didn't he also bring all the kingdoms together under the name 'England'? Perhaps he still liked being king of several kingdoms instead of just one – especially when he couldn't fight any battles to show off his power. Doesn't the folklore suggest he was the kind of man who wanted everyone to know he was the best?

AUTHOR'S SCORESHEET

POWER | 8 |

POPULARITY | 3 |

INFLUENCE ON WHAT CAME NEXT | 8 |

MAKER OF ENGLAND? | 7 |

YOUR SCORESHEET

POWER

POPULARITY

INFLUENCE ON WHAT CAME NEXT

MAKER OF ENGLAND?

EDWARD THE MARTYR

When Edgar died in AD 975, his eldest son Edward became the new king of the English.

According to the *Anglo-Saxon Chronicle*, as soon as Edward was crowned there was a comet in the sky, many farms turned to waste, and people grew restless all over the kingdoms. Were these signs from God that Edward's reign was going to end badly?

THE PUPPET KING

What did Edward do as a king? It's difficult to say — there aren't many facts to tell us. We don't even know how old he was when his father Edgar died, though historians guess he was a teenager.

We *do* know that some nobles really liked Edward — and others didn't. It's possible the nobles who *liked* Edward also told him what to do.

Even though Edward was king, maybe he wasn't the most powerful man in Britain. Armies from different English kingdoms, led by nobles, came close to fighting. It was almost like the Angles and Saxons had arrived all over again.

Fortunately, Edward didn't stay king for long. Unfortunately, that's because he was murdered.

FOLKLORE: THE MAKING OF A SAINT

Edward was Edgar's eldest son — but he wasn't Elfthryth's. She was his stepmother.

Elfthryth thought *her* son, Ethelred, should be the next king. And when the kingdoms started to fall apart during Edward's reign, she turned to some of the English nobles and said, 'I told you so.'

Some of those nobles asked her if she wanted to help them make Ethelred king. Elfthryth couldn't help but smile.

And of course she said, 'Yes.'

Like his father, Edward loved hunting. During a hunt in Wessex, a messenger arrived to invite Edward to drink at Corfe Hall nearby.

Edward was pleased for two reasons. First, hunting was thirsty work! And second, his stepmother lived at Corfe Hall. She was family – so it would be a safe place to go, right?

As Edward and his guards arrived at Corfe Hall, Elfthryth stood with a large goblet of mead in her hands, surrounded by guards and nobles – including Edward's half-brother, Ethelred. Edward told his guards to take a break – there was no point having *two* sets of guards on duty. Not here with his family. What could possibly go wrong?

Edward thanked his stepmum for the mead, took the goblet, and brought it to his lips. Suddenly he felt a sharp pain in his back, and tried to shout – but he just choked on the mead. That was the last thing he knew.

After removing the sword from his back, Elfthryth's guards lay Edward's dead body across the back of his horse. Then they knelt with Elfthryth and the nobles in front of Ethelred, and everyone said at once, 'Long live King Ethelred!'

*

News spread that King Edward was missing. No one said he'd been killed: Elfthryth, Ethelred and their friends certainly didn't tell anyone, and Edward's guards were all killed as well. So eventually, the rest of the English agreed that Ethelred should be king.

Elfthryth's guards threw Edward's body into a river near Corfe Hall. They were sure no one would find it there.

A little way along the river lived an old blind woman. Every day she used a stick to walk to the river, collect some water, then find her way home.

But one day when she got home, she suddenly saw a light. That's right – she *saw* a light! Her blindness had gone!

The woman thought she must be dreaming – because the light came in through the window, surrounding the floating body of King Edward.

Edward's body floated to lie on the woman's table. He was obviously dead, because he wasn't

moving or breathing. But there was also something magical about him: dead kings didn't normally float through windows!

Straight away, the woman ran into the nearby village to let everyone know what she'd seen.

The news soon spread beyond Wessex – even beyond Britain. People travelled huge distances to see the glowing body of the king. Some arrived on crutches, blind, or deaf – but they left able to walk, see, or hear again.

When Ethelred and Elfthryth heard the news, they pretended to be glad – but Elfthryth didn't like everyone's attention being on Edward. She wanted people to think *her* son was the blessed one! So she told Ethelred to bury Edward right away.

Ethelred did, and gave Edward a very expensive funeral. But people were already talking behind Ethelred's back, saying he had killed his half-brother to become king. They began calling Edward 'the Martyr', which meant he had suffered great pain to become a saint.

Edward's miracles kept happening even after Ethelred buried him. A spring burst through the ground outside the house of the ex-blind woman, so people could still travel from miles around to be cured of their ailments and diseases.

IS IT TRUE?

Most old books say Edward was killed while visiting Ethelred and Elfthryth. Some think he was killed by nobles, some by Elfthryth, and still others think Ethelred murdered him.

Beyond that, the story is told in many different ways. Sometimes Edward gets buried properly right after he's killed – though he still gets buried again later with a big ceremony paid for by Ethelred. Sometimes Elfthryth tries to burn down the house of the ex-blind woman. And sometimes it's said that Elfthryth became so evil that even her horse wouldn't go near her, so she had to walk everywhere for the rest of her life.

Whether or not the miracles at the ex-blind woman's house really happened, people certainly believed they did – and Edward became a saint. He is still celebrated today every 18th of March.

But does this folklore really tell us anything about Edward? He became holy after his death, but it doesn't say he was particularly religious *before* he died.

This story may be more of a clue that people didn't like Elfthryth or Ethelred. Which is a shame, because Ethelred was going to be king for longer than any other king in this book.

KING OF...?

Perhaps because he wasn't king for very long, Edward only ever really called himself 'King of the English'. He did try adding '...and surrounding nations' – but only once.

SUMMARY

On one hand, Edward seems to have pushed the English kingdoms apart again. The kingdoms began fighting once more towards the end of his reign, even though they all called Edward their king.

But after Edward's murder, men from every kingdom called him a martyr. Like the story of 'The Golden Apple', this could mean people moved between the kingdoms a lot more. So were the kingdoms becoming closer to uniting?

AUTHOR'S SCORESHEET

POWER | 3 *

POPULARITY | 10

INFLUENCE ON WHAT CAME NEXT | 6

MAKER OF ENGLAND? | 6

YOUR SCORESHEET

POWER

POPULARITY

INFLUENCE ON WHAT CAME NEXT

MAKER OF ENGLAND?

* AFTER HIS MURDER, ANYWAY

ETHELRED THE UNREADY

Like Alfred the Great, Ethelred became king after his brother died. But that's not the only similarity Ethelred shared with Alfred...

FOLKLORE: ETHELRED THE BROWN

Remember the story of 'The Man Who Would Be King', when Alfred's future was predicted by an important Christian? Well, something similar happened to Ethelred. Being a prince, Ethelred was baptised by the most important Christian in Britain: Archbishop Dunstan.

And, as Dunstan dipped baby Ethelred into the font...

Prrrppt!

Then a strange smell reached Dunstan's nose, and he screwed up his face in disgust!

Ethelred's Christening clothes were covered in smelly brown stains. The prince had just done a poo – right there in the holy water!

Dunstan held the baby up and said, '*Phwoar!* If this child gets to be king, he'll be thrown out by the Vikings!'

IS IT TRUE?

This story was first written down around 1129 by a historian called Henry of Huntingdon. Historians today think that Henry's books were a mixture of fact and folklore – like the book you're reading now! Though Henry didn't ask 'Is it true?' after *his* folklore...

Like 'The Making of a Saint', this story shows how much people disliked Ethelred. Facts show Dunstan certainly didn't like Ethelred as much as he liked Edward – that's why Dunstan crowned Edward first when Edgar died.

Of course, we also know that the prediction in the story came true...

NOT HIS FAULT?

Calling Ethelred 'the Unready' makes it look like he was a bad king. But when he was first given this name, it actually meant something different: 'Ethelred the Ill-Advised' – suggesting we should actually blame the nobles who advised Ethelred for all that went wrong during his reign.

However, we can't excuse Ethelred entirely. You see, *he* chose which nobles he listened to.

He ignored the nobles who advised Edgar and Edward. He obviously wasn't *ready* for good advice.

So 'Unready' seems a good word for him, with both the old meaning and the new!

TWO BAD

Ethelred actually had two goes at being king. His first was between 978 and 1013.

During that time, the Vikings began attacking again. If you had been one of Ethelred's nobles, what would you have advised? Train up the English armies like Alfred the Great had done?

Instead, Ethelred's nobles advised him to bribe the Vikings to leave England in peace. The Vikings must have liked this idea, because they went away very rich – carrying treasures they'd stolen *plus* treasures Ethelred gave them as a bribe!

In fact, we *know* the Vikings liked this idea – because, a few years later, they came back to do it again!

After bribing the Vikings a second time, Ethelred and his nobles realised their plan wasn't working: the Vikings would only return later to take more treasure and another bribe. But they also realised that the Vikings had help every time they came to Britain, from all the ordinary Viking people who lived in the English kingdoms. So they decided to kill all those ordinary Vikings.

Because they'd lived in the English kingdoms for so long, some of these Vikings now had English friends, or even English husbands or wives, so Ethelred's decision to kill all the Vikings wasn't very popular at home.

But it *really* wasn't popular in Denmark, as one of the Viking women killed by Ethelred's men had an important brother: Sweyn Forkbeard, King of Denmark (Harald Bluetooth's son).

Denmark was bigger, stronger, and more united than the English kingdoms – so when Sweyn attacked the English armies in 1004, he won every battle.

Quite a few Vikings got hurt too, so Sweyn returned to Denmark to recover – but he soon attacked the English again. A bribe wouldn't make Sweyn stop. He didn't just want treasure now. He wanted revenge.

And in 1013, he got it. Sweyn's Vikings defeated every English army, so Ethelred ran away to Normandy – leaving Sweyn to become king of the English. For about five weeks. Then, suddenly, Sweyn died. The English told Ethelred he could come back – but only if he *promised* to do better this time.

So Ethelred had another go at being king between 1014 and 1016, this time with new nobles advising him. Perhaps their advice was better, but Ethelred's old friends were now angry. This meant Ethelred didn't just have to worry about the Vikings – the English were fighting each other again too! And when Sweyn's son Knut brought a Viking army along in 1015, most of those kingdoms quickly agreed to call Knut their king.

In all that chaos during Ethelred's reign, though, you might have missed a significant step towards the beginning of England. Did you spot it? Before you read on, maybe have another quick read of this chapter so far.

SO, DID YOU?

Just a few pages ago, one paragraph began like this:

Ethelred's nobles advised him to bribe the Vikings to leave England in peace.

That's right! 'Leave *England*'! Ethelred's agreement with the Vikings was the first time the word England was used in a legal document!

So had Ethelred created England? Maybe. But Ethelred still wasn't calling himself 'King of England' – he still used 'King of the English'. Could there be another explanation? Well: remember how the Viking Harald Bluetooth stuck all *his* kingdoms together into one, and called it Denmark? The Vikings were used to seeing lots of smaller kingdoms, and thinking of them as a single big kingdom. Now those same Vikings were making an agreement with the English. If the Vikings saw all the English kingdoms as one big land called England, perhaps Ethelred called it that just to keep them happy?

KING OF...?

Others might have called him 'Unready', but Ethelred believed he deserved better than that. Sometimes he called himself 'King of the English' like his father had, but sometimes he called himself 'Emperor of Britain'! The kings in the north of Britain – which we now call Scotland – probably thought that was a bit cheeky.

Despite giving himself these fancy titles, though, Pope John wrote a letter to Ethelred in AD 991 calling him nothing more than 'King of the West Saxons'. Remember how Alfred had called himself that, but the Pope wrote Alfred a letter calling him 'King of the English'? It seems Ethelred was doing exactly the opposite: giving himself the grander title, and being cut down to size by the Pope!

SUMMARY

By the time Ethelred died in April 1016, he was already a bad guy in the folklore about his brother Edward. There's no other folklore about him, apart from that tale about his stinky Christening – and that doesn't make him look good either.

Ethelred was king for over thirty-five years – longer than anyone else in this book. But he wasn't the only leader in that time, and most of the kingdoms chose Knut to be their king before Ethelred died.

As we said a few paragraphs ago, Ethelred's reign was the exact opposite of Alfred's. Alfred brought the English together, beat the Vikings and brought peace to the land. Ethelred saw the English kingdoms divided again; he lost to the Vikings many times; and the English kingdoms were at war when he died. If nothing else, this meant Ethelred had a big impact on what would happen next. Killing Sweyn's sister along with all those ordinary Vikings, for example, may partly explain why Sweyn's son Knut brought an army to Britain – and will soon have a chapter in this book...

AUTHOR'S SCORESHEET

POWER   `4`
POPULARITY   `3`
INFLUENCE ON WHAT CAME NEXT   `10`
MAKER OF ENGLAND?   `4`

YOUR SCORESHEET

POWER   ☐
POPULARITY   ☐
INFLUENCE ON WHAT CAME NEXT   ☐
MAKER OF ENGLAND?   ☐

A FEW MORE MONKS

Let's take a little break from kings and queens for a few pages. Yes, they were important – and yes, they are some of the few people who had books written about them. But just as important were the men who did most of the writing: *the monks*.

Back at the beginning of this book, we met a monk called Bede – who may well have been the man who kickstarted the journey of the English people towards having a single kingdom, and all because he wrote a book. With the power of a pen, what else could a monk do?

ELFRIC: SMITHING FOR ENGLAND

You may remember, from our introduction, that one of the most important jobs an Anglo-Saxon or Viking could do was *blacksmithery*: making things out of metal. It may have been called 'black' because of the colour metal goes after being heated – or perhaps because of the thick black dust that would cover the worker as he hammered the metal beside a blazing hot fire. But the phrase 'smithery' simply means 'to work', and there are other kinds of smithery too – including *wordsmithery*.

During the reign of King Ethelred, one of the most famous wordsmiths was a monk called Elfric. At that time, most people could only understand the Bible if they knew how to read the language of Latin. Elfric is perhaps most famous for translating the Bible into English for the first time. It was still *Old* English – most people today would struggle to understand Elfric's writing. But back then, Elfric's work helped churches to tell stories in a language that everyone could understand, and that brought people together.

Elfric didn't just write Bible stories, though. He also wrote down tales about some of the saints. It's in some of these works that we see an Old English word for the first time:

Engla Lond

That's right: the best translation into today's English for this word would be *England*.

Before we get too excited, though, we should probably notice that the earliest copy of Elfric's work dates to around AD 1010. Being a copy, we can't be sure it was written by Elfric himself – after all, Elfric *died* around AD 1010. And if someone else copied it, *they* might have been the one who put in the word 'Engla Lond'.

But if anyone was going to invent the word 'England', doesn't it make sense that it would be a monk? After all, it was a monk who invented the idea of calling all Angles, Saxons and Jutes by the same name, *Angles*, which turned into 'English'. Both Bede and Alfred believed that being English meant you were a Christian living on the island of Britain. So perhaps a monk could take England to mean anywhere in Britain that you would find a Christian?

If so, the monks' idea of England could have been around at exactly the same time that the kings were still treating the kingdoms as separate lands like Mercia and Wessex.

But who would the *English people* have really listened to? The monks or the kings?

DUNSTAN: SMITHING FOR THE DEVIL

Already in this book, we've seen a king become a saint – even though that man, Edward, didn't do anything especially saintly in his life. So it probably makes more sense for a monk to become a saint, don't you think?

One medieval monk who did indeed become a saint was a man we've already met: the same Archbishop Dunstan who split up Edwy the Fair from his girlfriend, crowned Edgar the Peaceful, and smelt a strange whiff oozing up from the baptised baby Ethelred.

FOLKLORE: DUNSTAN'S TONGS

When Dunstan ran away to hide from Edwy, he decided to train up as a blacksmith. If Edwy ever tried looking for Dunstan, he was bound to send his soldiers to monasteries and churches first – so a blacksmith's workshop would be the perfect place to hide. Dunstan could even earn a few coins to buy himself food and drink!

Learning to be a blacksmith wasn't easy. The metal needed to be really, *really* hot before you could start to change its shape – so hot that you needed a long pair of tongs to hold it down on a solid metal table called an anvil. Then, to get it in the right shape, you had to hit it again and again with a hammer. It was tough work, but rewarding. After just a few weeks, Dunstan had made a spade for a farmer, a sword for a soldier, and even a patterned brooch for a lady's dress.

One day, Dunstan was hammering hard at the metal held between his tongs on his anvil – when in strolled a woman. And she was *beautiful!* Dunstan struggled to stay focused on his work; he had never seen anyone or anything so pretty in all his life. He could feel himself quickly falling in love.

But monks aren't supposed to have girlfriends – they're only supposed to love God – and even though Dunstan was *pretending* to be a blacksmith, he was determined to remain a monk at heart. So he kept looking at his piece of metal as he asked, 'How can I help you?'

Dunstan was surprised when a really deep, almost angry voice replied, 'I need a horseshoe. For me horse. Make one for me. Now.'

Now Dunstan looked at the woman – and saw there wasn't a woman at all. Instead there stood a fearsome-looking knight, who had muscles in his arms that were each as big as Dunstan's head.

The knight stepped forward and looked down at Dunstan with a menacing glare.

'You gonna do it or what?'

But monks aren't supposed to be scared – they're only supposed to be afraid of God – and even though Dunstan was *pretending* to be a blacksmith, he was determined to remain a monk at heart. So he looked back at his piece of metal as he said, 'I'm sorry, but I don't answer to threats.'

Dunstan was surprised when an elderly voice replied, 'Please, kind sir. I have a sack here that's full of gold, and it's all yours if you help me...'

Now Dunstan looked at the knight – and saw there wasn't a knight at all. Instead there stood an old man, who was holding open a large sack – a sack that really *was* full of glistening, gleaming, glorious gold!

But monks aren't supposed to be greedy – they're supposed to trust that God will bring them everything they need – and even though Dunstan was *pretending* to be a blacksmith, he was determined to remain a monk at heart. So Dunstan looked down at the old man's hooves and, shaking his head, said, 'I'm really sorry, I'm just too busy at the m—'

He suddenly stopped. The old man had hooves? Like... a *goat*?! With barely a second thought, Dunstan reached out and caught the old man's nose between the scorching hot metal points of his tongs.

The old man's eyes widened with surprise, his face went red with the pain, and horns burst out from his head.

It was the Devil! He wriggled his head and scratched at the tongs with his long claws, but the fiend could not writhe away from Dunstan's burning grip.

He screeched at Dunstan: '*Please let me go!*'

Dunstan held the tongs firm. 'Of course. But first, tell me: why are you here?'

The Devil hissed, and wriggled some more – but, since he still couldn't escape, he told Dunstan, 'I'm here to collect the souls of the people in this village!'

Now Dunstan shook his head. 'Oh no you're not. I command you to leave here, and never bother this village again. Do you understand me?'

The Devil nodded – as best he could with his nose still trapped in Dunstan's tongs. 'Yes, yes... I promise! Just let me go now, *please!*'

Dunstan smiled. 'Very well,' he said, and relaxed his grip.

As soon as the tongs opened, the Devil gave a loud wail and raced away from the workshop. He ran so fast he forgot all about his horse, and he was never seen in that village again. Everyone in that village went on to enjoy long, peaceful, and pain-free lives – and in fact, some say you'll have the same if you find that village yourself.

IS IT TRUE?

This story was first written down by another monk, Osbern of Canterbury, about 100 years after the story would have happened. So maybe – or maybe not.

Although not exactly the same, there are several other stories about blacksmiths who trick the Devil, including at least one more blacksmith who catches the Devil with his tongs. In fact, researchers at the University of Durham believe that the story of 'The Blacksmith and the Devil' is the oldest folk tale in the world!

But if people were telling this story about Dunstan so close to his life, it suggests he was a popular man – beating the Devil is definitely something done by heroes. And if monks were seen as heroes, maybe the English people would be ready to listen if a monk suggested everyone come together to form a new country called England?

WULFSTAN: SMITHING FOR KINGS

English *kings* certainly listened to the monks – especially the monks who became archbishops. Today, the job of archbishops is mainly to be the boss for many churches at once. But remember how Dunstan helped choose the next king, and was one of Edgar's favourite advisers? That was because medieval archbishops also helped make the law.

Wulfstan was Archbishop of York, and one of the advisers to Ethelred. Historians believe he wrote many of Ethelred's laws – and Wulfstan later wrote laws for the Viking king Knut, who'll have his own chapter soon.

Being Archbishop of York meant Wulfstan spent a lot of time in Northumbria, one of the last English kingdoms to have a Viking king. Even though Northumbria had been ruled by English kings since Eadred, many Vikings still lived there, and Wulfstan met them every day.

So perhaps you'd expect Wulfstan to start using some Viking words in his writing. And since we know that Vikings used the word 'England' in their treaty with Ethelred, perhaps it made sense for Wulfstan to use it too when writing laws for Knut?

SUMMARY

We can't know if Elfric really wrote the word 'England', or if Dunstan really fought the Devil, or even if it was Wulfstan's idea to put the word 'England' into Knut's laws. But Elfric's work translating Latin into English may have brought more English people together; Dunstan's legend shows that people thought monks were important, and Wulfstan's time in York may have given him a Viking influence.

Altogether, could they have helped make England as much as Bede did around 300 years earlier?

AUTHOR'S SCORESHEET

POWER   8

POPULARITY   8

INFLUENCE ON WHAT CAME NEXT   8

MAKER OF ENGLAND?   8

YOUR SCORESHEET

POWER

POPULARITY

INFLUENCE ON WHAT CAME NEXT

MAKER OF ENGLAND?

EDMUND IRONSIDE

Edmund Ironside didn't really get on with his dad Ethelred. Perhaps that's because everybody thought Ethelred was a weak king, whilst Edmund was described as a giant!

A LIFE OF WAR

Edmund was lucky to be so large, because most of his life was spent fighting. That's why people gave him the strong-sounding nickname 'Ironside'. He won many battles, even keeping Vikings out of London until Ethelred died in 1016.

But when he became king, Ironside had a problem. The Viking prince Knut had already taken over most of the other English kingdoms. Ironside's power already looked smaller than his father's – even though everyone thought Ironside was a stronger man! That didn't sound right – so Ironside trained an army to fight Knut's Vikings.

Ironside and Knut battled all over Britain, but their last battle was fought in East Anglia at a place called Assandun on the 18th of October 1016 – and Knut won.

But Knut didn't kill Ironside, nor even ask Ironside to call him overlord. Instead, Knut offered to become Ironside's brother – with Ironside being king of Wessex, and Knut being king of all the other English kingdoms. Knut also said that Ironside could be king of those kingdoms if Knut died first – but Knut would become king of Wessex if Ironside died first.

Why did Knut make this offer? Was he scared of Ironside? Or did he know the stories about Alfred the Great, and want to avoid Guthrum's mistake of invading Wessex?

Whatever Knut's reasons, Ironside accepted the offer. All he had to do was live longer than Knut, and he would rule all the English kingdoms.

Easy, right?

FOLKLORE: WIPEOUT

Ironside's sister, Edith, married a man called Eadric Streona, who was in charge of Mercia. Eadric and Ironside got on like true brothers, even though Eadric was only Ironside's brother-in-law. But this made it even more shocking when Eadric joined Knut's army in 1015.

Eadric helped Knut win many battles against Ironside. However, Ironside eventually managed to beat Eadric's men at a battle in Kent.

After that battle, Eadric begged Ironside for forgiveness. Because Eadric had been a good husband to his sister, Ironside forgave him – on one condition: that Eadric helped fight Knut.

Eadric agreed, and soldiers of Mercia were once again fighting alongside soldiers of Wessex.

Then came the Battle of Assandun on the 18th of October 1016. Ironside and Eadric's army faced Knut's Vikings over the fields. The Vikings charged – and, suddenly, Eadric's soldiers ran away!

Ironside and his soldiers were left to fight Knut alone. Perhaps that's why they lost, and Ironside agreed to keep himself to Wessex. Eadric, though, went back to being *Knut's* friend, helping the Vikings rule Mercia.

One day, Eadric found Knut pacing angrily around the great hall of his Mercian fortress. Knut had been told about the famous hunting forests in Wessex, and had sent messengers to Ironside asking if he could visit them. But Ironside had sent a reply saying, 'Not yet – maybe after Christmas.'

Knut didn't see Eadric – in fact, he thought he was alone, and started talking to himself: 'Ironside has such a cheek! He's just showing off that he has the best hunting grounds in Britain. I should have him killed – then *I'd* be king of Wessex! Ha! Oh, if someone could get rid of Ironside for me, I'd put that man higher than any other man in Britain.'

Knut then stormed off. He still hadn't noticed Eadric.

Eadric smiled. He liked the idea of being higher than any other man in Britain.

Eadric went to visit his brother-in-law on the 30th of November 1016. Ironside was grumpy with Eadric at first, but – after some brotherly chit-chat – they were like a family again. Ironside even invited Eadric to stay for dinner.

During the meal, Ironside excused himself to go to the toilet – which in those days was called a privy: a hut built over a hole in the ground.

When someone knocked on the privy door, Ironside said, 'This one's busy.'

Suddenly the door burst open. Confused, Ironside looked up – and saw Eadric taking aim with a bow.

Eadric's arrow went straight through Ironside's heart. Ironside couldn't even shout – he breathed his last.

Nobody noticed Eadric slip back into the dining hall. No one even worried about Ironside until he missed pudding. A guard went to check the privy – and returned in horror.

Soon everybody knew that Ironside was dead. Word was sent to Knut to let him know: he was now king of Wessex, too.

Knut hurried to the fortress where Ironside's body had been laid on a table for his friends to say goodbye. Eadric was there, looking forward to claiming his reward from Knut.

But when Knut saw Ironside, he burst into tears and hugged the body, saying, 'Oh, my brother...'

Eadric wasn't expecting that. Knut looked genuinely upset about Ironside's death. So Eadric decided he wouldn't ask for his reward just yet.

Knut paid for Ironside to have a huge funeral. He even refused to be called king of Wessex until the new year.

Eadric waited a whole year before letting Knut know he killed Ironside. In the middle of the party for Christmas 1017, Eadric sat next to a jolly Knut.

'So, your Majesty, do you enjoy hunting in Wessex whenever you want?'

Knut nodded. 'Yes! I feel like I'm part of the family of Alfred the Great!'

Eadric felt the conversation was going well. 'Do you remember you once said you'd put a man higher than any other man in Britain if he helped you get to hunt in those forests?'

Knut raised an eyebrow. 'You mean, if a man got rid of Ironside for me...'

Eadric beamed. 'Yes! That was me! And now it's Christmas, your Majesty, I thought you might like to show me what it means to be higher than everyone else?'

The joy disappeared from Knut's face. He slowly got to his feet. 'Certainly – I'll show you...'

*

As the executioner raised the axe above Eadric's terrified head, Knut declared

that Eadric had been a traitor to his own brother-in-law, the great Ironside.

After the chop, though, Knut kept his promise. Eadric's head was put on a spike and placed higher than any other man in Britain...

IS IT TRUE?

Several ancient books mention Eadric's betrayals of Ethelred, Ironside, Knut, then Ironside again – but it wasn't until Henry of Huntingdon that anyone wrote about Ironside being killed in the privy. Remember: parts of Henry's history books are folklore, but he doesn't always say which ones.

Other ancient books tell us that Knut had Eadric's head chopped off. The writer of Knut's life story, writing about five years after Knut died, says that Knut was angry with Eadric for betraying Ironside – but he doesn't mention Eadric *killing* Ironside. In fact, he doesn't mention Ironside's murder at all. Ironside might have died naturally.

This folklore tells us that people hated Eadric. But it also shows that people quite liked Ironside *and* Knut. Knut appears to be compassionate, while Ironside is shown to be so strong that he could only be killed when at his most vulnerable – on the toilet!

KING OF...?

You might expect Ironside to go back to being 'King of the West Saxons', as Alfred had been before the English kings started ruling the lands beyond Wessex. But actually, Ironside chose a much more sneaky title: 'the Son of the English and the surrounding nations'.

In this way, Ironside may have tried to keep some of the honour his father had for ruling all of the English and those surrounding nations – without admitting that he'd lost it all to Knut...

SUMMARY

Despite being a huge man, Ironside couldn't keep control of all the English kingdoms. After he died, every kingdom that had ever been created by the English was ruled over by a Viking.

But is he still an England-maker? After all, his agreement with Knut is what led to the Vikings finally taking control of the last English kingdom.

Plus, one of Ironside's sons was another Edward, known as 'the Exile'. This Edward would never be king, but he did have an important role in the future of England. We'll learn about that soon.

AUTHOR'S SCORESHEET

POWER   7
POPULARITY   7
INFLUENCE ON WHAT CAME NEXT   9
MAKER OF ENGLAND?   4

YOUR SCORESHEET

POWER
POPULARITY
INFLUENCE ON WHAT CAME NEXT
MAKER OF ENGLAND?

KNUT THE GREAT

By now, we've seen it wasn't unusual for the kings in Britain to fight for power over the seven English kingdoms.

At first, Knut was exactly the same. He fought Ethelred's armies alongside his father, Sweyn Forkbeard, in 1013, when he was probably only a teenager. Then, in 1015, he brought his own Viking army to Britain, and quickly encouraged every English kingdom except Wessex to call him king.

Did Knut really ask for Ironside to be murdered? We'll never know for sure. After Ironside died, though, Knut became the first Viking to rule *all* the English kingdoms.

KNUT THE CONQUEROR

After becoming king of all the English, Knut wanted to make sure no one else tried to take over from him. So he ordered his men to kill a few powerful Englishmen – such as Eadric Streona.

But it soon became obvious that Knut wanted to be a better king than Ethelred. For starters, he didn't kill any princes or princesses: instead, he sent Ethelred and Ironside's children away to live in countries across the sea.

Not only that, but Knut paid most of his Viking soldiers to go away too! Ethelred had *bribed* the Vikings away, which is probably why they kept returning. Knut didn't need to bribe them: he could just ask them to leave, giving them money for their hard work helping him to become king, and that was it. There were no more battles between the English and the Vikings until thirty years after Knut died.

Fifty years later, William the Conqueror took over – and did everything he could to make sure people knew the Normans were in charge. But even though Knut was a Viking, he seemed happy to let many Englishmen keep their important jobs – including Archbishop Wulfstan, who kept his job helping to make laws.

Knut also gave gifts to English churches, and got baptised as a Christian – even though no one forced him to do this, like Alfred forced Guthrum.

THE ORIGINAL MAGNA CARTA

Two hundred years before King John agreed to the famous Magna Carta, Knut passed almost exactly the same law: 'that impartial justice may be enjoyed by all, noble and common'.

If you remember our introduction, we mentioned how King John never actually liked his Magna Carta – in fact, he started fighting his nobles only a few days later. Knut, on the other hand, really wanted this law. He wrote it in a letter to his nobles, and he obeyed this law himself.

The only reason Knut's law didn't last long was because William the Conqueror and his Normans got rid of it. William wanted the law to say he and his Normans could do anything they liked!

THE LAW OF... ENGLAND!

Ethelred's treaty with the Vikings might have been the first time the word 'England' was used in an official document, but that document didn't really matter to most people. It was really just an agreement between Ethelred and the Vikings. But Knut *was* a Viking. And when he issued his laws, they were the first laws to say they were for 'all his subjects in *England*'. He even introduced some of his laws by calling himself 'King of All England' – and just to be sure, he had this written in both Latin *and* Old English.

So it seemed a king was finally ready to call all the kingdoms by one single name: *England*.

Why did he do this? Because Archbishop Wulfstan suggested it? Because his grandfather, Harald Bluetooth, did the same thing with Denmark a few years earlier? Or was it because Knut believed this was a way to stop his people fighting each other?

Calling his kingdom England meant that everybody living there could feel like part of the same team: the English from all over Britain, Knut's Vikings, and even Vikings who had lived there since Alfred's time. Because they could all say they lived in England, they could now *all* say they were English.

It might have been for some of these reasons, or it might have been for all of them. There sadly aren't any facts to tell us for sure. No record survives of the date that Knut first called his kingdom England. All we have are his laws and letters – plus the *Anglo-Saxon Chronicle*, which also uses the words 'King of England' for the *first time* when it describes Knut.

FOLKLORE: KNUT AND THE WAVES

After Knut had been king for a while, England started doing very well. People paid plenty of taxes to send the Viking soldiers home, that's true. However, because they weren't spending so much money on bribes – and because nobody was stealing their treasure – people soon recovered. Some even became richer than before.

It wasn't long before nearly everybody was grateful to Knut, and called him the most powerful ruler they'd ever had.

If a church roof was falling down, the priests often sent a message to Knut to let him know – and Knut sent money to repair it. Anyone who saw a hole in a church roof began to say, 'Don't worry, Knut will fix that!'

If fishermen struggled to get food, they often sent a message to Knut to let him know – and Knut sent them food from another part of the kingdom. Anyone with an empty fishnet began to say, 'Don't worry, Knut will fix that!'

And if farmers noticed that the rain hadn't watered their crops for a while, and they were getting hungry, they began to say, 'Don't worry, Knut will fix that!'

Knut grew concerned. He met with his nobles and said, 'People are beginning to think I can do anything! They expect me to make it rain! What can I do?'

All the nobles smiled reassuringly and said, 'Don't worry, your Majesty – you will fix that!'

Knut put his head in his hands.

Later that day, Knut prayed in his chapel. 'Please, God – tell me how I can show people that I can't do everything!'

As if in answer, an idea popped into Knut's head.

Soon afterwards, Knut assembled his nobles by the seaside. He even commanded his soldiers to bring his throne and place it right by the edge of the water. A crowd of ordinary people gathered to watch.

Knut addressed them all. 'My good people! I will show you exactly how powerful I am! Watch and learn.'

Then he sat on his throne, turned to the sea, and said, 'I command you, waters: turn away!'

Everybody waited excitedly. Their king was going to perform a miracle!

The water, though, didn't move away just yet. In fact, the tide was coming in – soon the water began lapping at Knut's feet.

Knut raised his arms and called out louder: 'I command you, waters: turn away!'

A few people changed their enthusiastic faces for curious faces. It seemed the water wasn't listening to Knut. The tide continued to come in, and the waves gradually washed past the throne.

Knut raised his arms even higher, and gave a deep, strong bellow: 'Waters! I command you! Go away **now!**'

Everyone waited to see what the waters would do. Would the tide go out? Would the waves stop? Would the sea leave the country entirely?

None of these things happened. Instead, the tide kept coming in as it always did. The waves splashed past Knut's throne, now covering the legs of the nobles too.

Knut could see his nobles beginning to shiver from the chilly water around their feet – yet their

cheeks were rosy with embarrassment. They had realised their mistake.

Now Knut stood up and addressed the crowds. 'Let this be a lesson to us all! There are some things that men cannot do – not even kings! There is only one master of everything in this world.'

With that, Knut waded across the beach to a nearby church. Inside, he found a picture of Jesus – and, above that picture, Knut hung his crown. He never wore it himself again.

From that day on, everyone agreed that Knut was the strongest, kindest, *wisest* king they'd ever had.

But from then on they stopped sending him quite so many messages to fix things...

IS IT TRUE?

Like the folklore of Ethelred and Ironside, we first see this story in a book written by Henry of Huntingdon – a historian who put facts and folklore beside each other, but didn't say which was which.

The story has been told all over the country, too. Henry seemed to think this event happened at a seaside. Other historians think that, if it did happen, it must have happened by the River Thames in London, not by the sea. There's also a sign in Southampton (a town with a popular beach) that says the story happened there, in exactly 1028. Still other historians and storytellers say the tale took place in Lincolnshire, Cheshire and others!

It's strange, though, that Henry is the first writer to mention it, since he was writing in 1129. If Knut really made everybody feel silly with such a grand stunt, surely others would have written about it? It wasn't even mentioned in Knut's life story, which was written only five years after Knut died.

Then again, maybe no one *wanted* to talk about it. After all, Knut made them look silly!

ANOTHER POINT OF VIEW?

In recent years (from Victorian times to today), some people have seen the story of 'Knut and the Waves' differently. They say Knut actually thought he *could* tell the tides to change. Instead of describing Knut as wise, people say he must have been arrogant, proud and foolish.

But what did people think in Knut's time? Although Henry of Huntingdon calls Knut 'graceful and magnificent', that could just be because Knut put his crown above a picture of Jesus. And remember, Henry was writing around 100 years later.

Let's see what other folklore tells us...

FOLKLORE: SAND IN HIS SHOE

About 15 miles south of Manchester is a town called Knutsford. Every year on the first of May, the people of the town throw coloured sand on their streets.

This all began shortly after Knut became king. He was travelling north to meet the kings of Scotland, and had to pass a river along the way. Because there was no bridge, Knut and his men waded through the water – and came out the other side soaking wet, with sand in their boots.

At that same moment, a newly married couple were just leaving a church with their families and friends. When they saw the king and his men, everyone in the wedding party stopped and gasped.

Knut was just about to tip out the grains of sand from his boot when he noticed everything had gone quiet. He looked up at the bride and her new husband, and smiled. Then he shook the sand out from his boot, saying, 'I wish you every blessing – and that your new family gets to be as big as the number of grains falling from my boot!'

Everyone laughed and the couple thanked Knut, inviting the king and his men to their reception.

IS IT TRUE?

The people of Knutsford certainly think so! That's why they still celebrate the story by throwing coloured sand around – and, in fact, that's why they called their town 'Knutsford'!

And it *could* have happened. Knutsford is along one of the routes you can take from Wessex to Scotland, and Knut did travel to visit the Scottish kings a few times.

Whether or not it actually happened, it gives us another clue that *English people liked him.* Knutsford is in Cheshire, which used to be part of the English side of Mercia. Folklore only survives if it's popular – so for this story to survive, Knut must have been popular with the English.

FOLKLORE: THE EEL CATCHER'S DAUGHTER

At first, though, Knut knew the English didn't like him much. After all, Viking soldiers had killed many English soldiers. So Knut wanted to know how to be a good king for the English. To learn, he disguised himself as an English farmer so he could get close to ordinary English people.

One day, Knut was in his disguise, trudging through the marshes near a river in Cambridgeshire, when it began to get dark. He knew it was dangerous to travel through the marshes at night: you could accidentally slip, fall and drown!

Fortunately, Knut spotted a hut on his side of the river. He strode up to it and knocked on the door.

The door opened and an Englishman looked out with a frown. 'What do you want?'

Knut bowed. 'Kind sir. My name is Edmund, a farmer. I started my journey home late. I'm worried about walking in the marshes at night. Please can I stay with you until morning?'

The man raised an eyebrow, but said, 'I suppose you can stay for one night. You can eat dinner with us too, if you like.'

Knut was glad, and made a note in his mind to send a big thank you gift to this home when he returned to his fortress in Wessex.

Inside the house sat a boy wearing a cap, polishing a spear. The boy gave Knut a wary look, then went back to his polishing.

The man showed Knut inside. 'My name's Legres, and this here's my son, Ethelred. I'm just cooking our dinner: eel stew. You can eat with us if you like.'

As Legres stirred a pot full of eels, Knut sat next to Ethelred. 'Hello.'

Ethelred didn't answer.

Knut didn't get angry; he knew children were shy sometimes. He noticed the spear that Ethelred was polishing, which had several extra pointy bits on the end.

'What's that?'

Ethelred didn't answer.

'Hmm,' said Knut. 'Is it... a comb for hairy toes?'

This time, Ethelred laughed. 'No, silly. It's an eel spear.'

'Ah,' said Knut. 'Your dad's an eel catcher?'

Ethelred nodded proudly. 'I'll be an eel catcher too, when I grow up.'

Knut was happy to see the boy cheer up. 'Is your mum around?'

The boy's smile disappeared, and he looked down.

Legres interrupted. 'His mum's gone. End of story.'

And that nearly *was* the end of the story. Knut enjoyed the eel stew, but Legres and Ethelred didn't talk much. After dinner, everyone lay down on a rug and went to sleep. In the morning, Knut awoke to find that Ethelred was out, and Legres was still asleep.

Knut stepped outside for some fresh air – and suddenly heard the sound of a girl singing near the river. Whoever she was, she sang beautifully! Knut wanted to thank her for giving him such a lovely start to his day. Knut crept carefully towards the river – he didn't want to surprise the girl when he found her, in case she slipped and fell into the marshes.

However, it was Knut who got the surprise. The singer was Ethelred!

Ethelred stood in the river, using the fork-spear to catch eels. But that voice was definitely a girl's voice. Knut also saw some long hair tumbling out of Ethelred's cap.

Why had Legres disguised his daughter as a son? Knut decided to find out. He stepped forward and coughed.

Ethelred spun round and gasped.

'Shhh…' said Knut. 'I'm not going to hurt you, I promise. I see you have a secret. Well, I have a secret too …'

Knut pulled his crown from his sack, and placed it on his head. The girl gave another gasp – but she wasn't afraid this time, she was amazed. Knut explained why he was pretending to be a farmer. Then the girl sat with Knut on the riverbank. She started by telling Knut her real name: Ethel!

'You see, your majesty, some monks living nearby like to steal women and make them slaves. They stole Mum, so Dad disguised me as a boy to stop them taking me as well!'

Knut was amazed. Monks were doing this? Monks were supposed to be Christians! Knut hadn't been a Christian for long, but he already knew that Christians weren't supposed to steal women and make them slaves.

'Ethel, I think we need to teach those monks a lesson. But first, let's speak with your father...'

At first, Legres was angry when he saw that Ethel had taken off her cap to show off her long hair. But when he saw the shining crown on Knut's head, Legres bowed.

Now Knut understood why Legres and Ethel had been sad and suspicious when he arrived – Legres had lost his wife, and Ethel had lost her mum! But Knut had a plan.

'Legres,' he said, 'are your wife's clothes still here?'

Legres nodded.

'Good,' said Knut. 'Now, take this letter to my soldiers in Ely – the wax seal will prove that I sent you. Go now, and we'll see you again soon.'

Once Legres left, Knut turned to Ethel. 'You and I will visit the abbey where those monks live. But first, I need to change my clothes...'

A little while later, Ethel took Knut to the monastery, all the way trying hard not to giggle. Why? Well, not because Knut wore her mother's dress. It wasn't because he wore a wig either, held on with a comb. No: it was because he hadn't had time to shave! So he looked a very strange woman indeed...

When they got close to the monastery, Knut winked at Ethel. 'They must find us quickly, or my plan won't work. So you have an important job now: sing as loud as you can!'

Ethel blushed at first – she didn't think she was very good. But soon, with Knut's encouragement, she began a first verse, and was soon singing as loudly, confidently, and as beautifully as she had been by the river.

Suddenly, the thick wooden doors of the monastery swung open. Some monks rushed out, caught Ethel and Knut, and led them into the monastery. Inside, unhappy women were sweeping corridors, cleaning windows, carrying water, and doing all sorts of other jobs – all while dragging heavy chains attached to their legs. But the monks sat around chuckling and burping, and jeered at Knut and Ethel as they were brought in.

Sitting in a grand chair was the Abbott, the leader of the monks. He poked his tongue out at Knut.

'What an ugly old woman! I know what your job will be. You can dust the bell tower. No one will care if the dust covers your face!'

Then the Abbott looked at Ethel. 'Hmm. What job could this little scallywag do?'

One monk suggested, 'This girl was singing beautifully, Abbott. Maybe we could put her in a cage, and make her sing for us like a bird!'

The Abbott laughed. 'What a good idea!'

Knut put on a really high voice. 'You'll never get away with this! What if King Knut finds out?'

The Abbott laughed louder. 'King Knut? He will never know about us. People are too scared to say anything, and even if they did – King Knut is a Christian. Everyone *knows* monks are Christians. Why would the king believe anyone trying to tell him monks are behaving badly?'

Now it was Knut's turn to grin.

'Because... he's *here*!' Moving swiftly, Knut pulled out the comb from his hair. The wig fell away to reveal his crown. The monks gasped. Some fell to their knees and begged Knut for forgiveness.

But the Abbott just sneered, 'You're all alone, king. What can you possibly do here?'

Just then, the doors burst open, and in came a hundred Viking soldiers on horses! They began tying up the monks with rope. The Abbott tried to run, but some of the slave women rushed to get in his way – so the Vikings caught him easily.

Seeing Legres on one of the horses, Ethel ran over to him. 'Daddy!' As they hugged, one of the slave women came up and tapped Ethel on her shoulder. Ethel turned round, and gasped. '*Mummy!*'

One Viking dragged the Abbott to Knut. 'What should we do with these monks, your majesty?'

Knut mused. 'Well, I've heard a few interesting ideas... But let me ask one of my royal advisers...' He called to Ethel. 'Young lady – what do *you* think we should do with these monks?'

Ethel thought for a moment, then said: 'These monks liked making women into slaves, so I think you should make *them* into slaves. They should be forced to build a whole village for us to live in!'

And do you know what? That's exactly what Knut did. The monks were forced to build a village, which you can still visit today: its name is Littleport.

IS IT TRUE?

This story comes from Cambridgeshire, a county in the old kingdom of East Anglia. It was first written down by a man called Walter Barrett in 1963, but was told by storytellers before then. One storyteller even said he was related to Legres.

There's no record of any monks kidnapping women. But then, who wrote nearly all the records in those days? Monks! However, there *are* records by the monks of Ely, a city in Cambridgeshire, which say that Knut got upset with them and wanted to throw them out of their monastery – though they don't say why. Were the monks trying to hide their naughtiness from becoming historical fact? (The same thing is recorded by some monks in a nearby place called Ramsay – perhaps *that* is where Knut rescued the eel catcher's wife?)

Whatever the truth, here we have yet another example of Knut being popular with the English.

FOLKLORE: QUEEN EMMA'S HONOUR

Our final tale begins after Knut's death – but it might still say something about him. The heroine of this story is actually his wife, Queen Emma.

Emma came from Normandy to be the wife of Ethelred the Unready, and had a son called Edward. But after Ethelred and Ironside had died, Knut asked Emma to be *his* wife. They had their own son together: Hardeknut.

Not long after Knut died in 1035, his son Hardeknut became king of England. Edward was only allowed to take over when Hardeknut died in 1042. He would become known as 'the Confessor' because he spent a lot of time in church (confessing is one of the things people often go to church to do).

But Edward had a few Norman friends – including a bishop called Robert. Edward asked Robert to be Archbishop of Canterbury – the most important job in the English Church. Edward trusted everything Robert said. There was just one problem: Robert *really* didn't like Emma.

In fact, none of the Normans did, ever since Emma had married Knut. They were especially upset with Emma for letting Hardeknut become king before Edward – and so Robert hatched a plan to teach Emma a lesson.

One day Robert told Edward, 'Your Majesty! Your mother has been accused of being a witch!'

At first, Edward just laughed. But because Robert sounded so sure – and because Edward trusted his Norman friend – Edward was soon convinced. 'What can I do?'

'It's simple, your Majesty. We must put your mother to a witch trial: she must walk across some red-hot plough blades. If she crosses without getting burned, we'll know she's innocent. But if the blades scald her, then we'll have to kill her!'

Now, I ask you: are you a witch or wizard who flies on a broomstick? I'm guessing you're probably not. But if you touched something red-hot, would your skin burn? Of course it would!

So Robert's test was unfair – and he knew it. He *wanted* Emma to fail. But because Edward believed Robert was a good Christian, he didn't suspect the archbishop of trickery. He summoned his mother and told her about the trial.

Emma's eyes widened. 'My son! You're surely not asking me to walk across red-hot blades!'

Edward refused to let his face show any care. 'No, mother. I'm *ordering* you to walk across red-hot blades. If you don't, then we'll know you're a witch even without the trial.'

Tears fell from Emma's eyes. 'At least let me visit the chapel to pray.'

Robert sneered. 'Witches don't pray.'

But Edward held up his hand. 'We haven't proved she's a witch yet, Archbishop, so she can pray in the chapel. But I'll send some guards with her.'

A little while later, Emma knelt in front of an altar. She decided to pray to St Swithun. 'Good saint: you spent hours walking for the glory of God. Please let my feet walk for his glory too – and show my innocence!'

When Emma returned to the great hall, some plough blades were being heated in the fireplace. Emma gulped as the guards used large tongs to pick up the red-hot blades and line them up on the ground in front of her.

'Now,' said Robert. 'Cross, witch!'

Emma closed her eyes, hitched up her dress, and stepped forward.

She took another step. And another.

She kept walking in a straight line. She couldn't hear any talking, just the hissing of the hot blades on the wooden floor – but she couldn't feel

anything either. Confused, she stood still. 'Can someone tell me how far away the blades are?'

She heard a chorus of gasps, followed by her son's voice.

'Mother – you're standing on them!'

Emma opened her eyes. He was right! She'd nearly crossed the red-hot blades without even feeling them!

Robert demanded to inspect her feet, but he couldn't find any burn marks at all.

Edward was pleased to prove his mother wasn't a witch, and promised her he would never ask her to do anything like that again. But Edward also realised he couldn't trust Robert anymore, and sent him back to Normandy – threatening to chop off his head if he ever returned to England.

Afterwards, Emma went straight to the church of St Swithun in Winchester (now known as Winchester Cathedral), and gave the priests many expensive gifts to thank the saint for his help.

IS IT TRUE?

Archbishop Robert of Jumièges was certainly a Norman friend of Edward the Confessor – until they suddenly fell out in 1052 and he was exiled to Normandy. But most historians think this is because Robert had a problem with Edward's father-in-law Godwin, who had also been a good friend of Knut.

Still, Emma certainly gave many fine gifts to Winchester Cathedral, and in 2019 archaeologists discovered that Emma had been buried there. Was this because she owed her life to St Swithun?

Again, the story wasn't written down until a long time after the characters had died – as much as 300 years later! But as well as being passed down by storytellers, historians have found copies of a song written to tell this story too.

Here's what this story tells us: the English didn't like Robert, but they were happy with Emma. And if they were happy with her, they were probably happy with her husband Knut, too.

KING OF...?

As we've seen, Knut's laws and letters described him as 'King of England', and he's the first king to be given that title in the *Anglo-Saxon Chronicle*. So: case closed?

Well... Not quite. Like the other English kings before him, Knut spent a lot of time travelling the country to put his name on *charters* – special documents that people could use to prove that they owned land, buildings and so on. And, oddly, Knut doesn't use the title 'King of England' in *any* of these.

Instead, he uses 'King of the English', or even 'King of the Whole of Britain'. That last one is just as cheeky as when Ethelred used it, because the north of the island was still under the control of the people who would become Scottish.

If Knut wanted everyone to feel part of a new united country of England, why didn't he use his new title everywhere? Perhaps it's simply because he didn't write those charters, he only *watched* them get written – and the writers were probably used to making them up for the old English kings.

Or maybe it's because charters were for the rich, and rich people can sometimes be the slowest to accept change – after all, the old ways helped them to make their money! The laws, though, were for everyone, and Knut wanted everyone to think of the land as 'England'.

Whatever the reason, we *can* still rest our case with Knut. That's because the earliest evidence we have for him being 'King of England' dates from around 1050 – not long after he had died, but before William the Conqueror arrived in 1066. So we have plenty of proof that Knut was the first king to ever be called 'King of England', even before the Norman invasion.

SUMMARY

Why did Knut make laws for a land called England? Did he want to end the hatred between English and Vikings that led to the death of his aunt? Was it because he became a Christian? Or was it because he made friends with ordinary English folk like Legres and Ethel?

All we can say for sure is that the Normans didn't want people to remember Knut or his laws – they tried to pretend he never existed. But ordinary people remembered Knut with their stories about him, so he must have meant a lot to them.

And if those stories can be believed, England meant a lot to Knut, too.

AUTHOR'S SCORESHEET

POWER   10

POPULARITY   9

INFLUENCE ON WHAT CAME NEXT   9

MAKER OF ENGLAND?   9

YOUR SCORESHEET

POWER

POPULARITY

INFLUENCE ON WHAT CAME NEXT

MAKER OF ENGLAND?

WHAT HAPPENED NEXT?

Back in the introduction, we saw how Queen Elizabeth II is the great-great-(etc.)-granddaughter of William the Conqueror, the Norman bully who managed to convince historians for a long time that he was the first important king of England.

But remember Ironside? I briefly mentioned one of his sons: Edward the Exile. This Edward was never a king in Britain, but his daughter Margaret got to be a queen: she married King Malcolm of Scotland.

Malcolm and Margaret had a daughter called Matilda, who married one of William the Conqueror's sons: King Henry I.

Because Matilda was the granddaughter of Edward the Exile, she was the great-granddaughter of Ironside – and the great-great-great-great-great-great-granddaughter of? *Alfred the Great*.

So Queen Elizabeth II is also related to one of the great English kings before William!

Her Majesty is not related to King Knut. However, Knut affected English history more than he probably realised. Not only was he the first king to be called 'King of England', but his laws were used by King Henry II (William the Conqueror's great-grandson) to help create the *English Common Law*. This is the law of the courts in England, and is the foundation for most of the legal systems in the world today.

He also sent the sons of Ethelred and Ironside to other countries like Normandy and Sweden. This is why Edward the Confessor made Norman friends – one of whom became William the Conqueror. It's also how Edward the Exile survived to become Queen Elizabeth II's great-great-(etc.)-grandfather.

In many ways, though, *all* of these kings, queens and monks helped create England. Now that you know their stories, will they have an impact on you too?

Will you learn from Ethelred and try to get the best advice before making a decision?

Will you be like Alfred and Ethelfled and try to be as good at reading and writing as you are at sport?

Will you be like Bede and Knut, who saw that people from different places and cultures are stronger when they work together?

What do you want to come next for *your* country?

BIBLIOGRAPHY

Barrett, W.H., *Tales from the Fens* (Routledge & Kegan Paul, 1963)

Bilbé, T. & England, D., *Berkshire Folk Tales* (The History Press, 2013)

Dacre, M., *Devonshire Folk Tales* (The History Press, 2014)

East, H., *London Folk Tales* (The History Press, 2012)

Flude, K., *Divorced, Beheaded, Died...* (Michael O'Mara Books, 2009)

Foot, S., *Æthelstan: The First King of England* (Yale University Press, 2012)

Jacksties, S., *Somerset Folk Tales* (The History Press, 2012)

Journey Man, The, *Cheshire Folk Tales* (The History Press, 2014)

Keynes, S., *Alfred the Great: Asser's Life of King Alfred* (Penguin, 2004)

Pollard, J., *Alfred the Great: The Man Who Made England* (John Murray, 2006)

Robertson, A.J., *The Laws of the Kings of England from Edmund to Henry I* (Cambridge University Press, 1925)

Robinson, T., *Kings and Queens* (Red Fox, 2014)

Skeat, W. W., *Aelfric's Lives of Saints* (Early English Text Society, 1881)

Swanton, M., *The Anglo-Saxon Chronicles* (Phoenix Press, 2000)

Trow, M.J., *Cnut: Emperor of the North* (Sutton Publishing, 2005)

Whitelock, D., *English Historical Documents, c.500–1042* (Eyre & Spottiswoode, 1955)

Wood, M., *In Search of England* (Penguin Books, 2000)

—, *The Great Turning Points in British History* (Constable, 2009)

Wormald, P., *Engla Londe: The Making of an Allegiance* (Journal of Historical Sociology, March 1994)

Society *for*
Storytelling

Since 1993, the Society for Storytelling has championed the art of oral storytelling and the benefits it can provide – such as improving memory more than rote learning, promoting healing by stimulating the release of neuropeptides, or simply great entertainment! Storytellers, enthusiasts and academics support and are supported by this registered charity to ensure the art is nurtured and developed throughout the UK.

Many activities of the Society are available to all, such as locating storytellers on the Society website, taking part in our annual National Storytelling Week at the start of every February, purchasing our quarterly magazine *Storylines*, or attending our Annual Gathering – a chance to revel in engaging performances, inspiring workshops, and the company of like-minded people.

You can also become a member of the Society to support the work we do. In return, you receive free access to *Storylines*, discounted tickets to the Annual Gathering and other story-telling events, the opportunity to join our mentorship scheme for new storytellers, and more. Among our great deals for members is a 30% discount off titles in the *Folk Tales* series from The History Press website.

For more information, including how to join, please visit

www.sfs.org.uk